FEARLESS

Building a Faith That Overcomes your Fear

Cheri Fuller

FEARLESS

Building a Faith That Overcomes your Fear

Cheri Fuller

Fleming H. Revell
A Division of Baker Book House Co
Grand Rapids, Michigan 49516

Published by Fleming H. Revell
a division of Baker Book House Company
P.O. Box 6287, Grand Rapids, MI 49516-6287
www.bakerbooks.com

Printed in the United States of America

Library of Congress Cataloging-in-Publication Data
Fuller, Cheri.
    Fearless : building a faith that overcomes your fear / Cheri Fuller.
       p.   cm.
    Includes bibliographical references.
    ISBN 0-8007-5854-4 (pbk.)
    1. Christian women—Religious life. 2. Fear—Religious aspects—Christianity. I. Title.
BV4527.F845 2003
248.8′6—dc21   2003007209

To Alison
Through your life and faith, God has filled me with wonder
and gratitude. The adventurous spirit with which you pursue
life inspires me to press on to follow him.

The Lord your God is with you,
He is mighty to save.
He will take great delight in you,
He will quiet you with his love,
He will rejoice over you with singing.
Zephaniah 3:17

Contents

Acknowledgments

Thank you, Vicki Crumpton, for catching a vision for this book and for your editorial wisdom and encouragement. Thank you to the outstanding staff at Revell—it is a delight to work with you.

Heartfelt thanks to Dana Iverson for her help, dedication, and heart for God's Word in cowriting the new discussion guide and Bible study. And to Louise Tucker Jones, I am grateful for your help, questions, and contributions to the original study guide.

Thank you, Connie Willems, for your insight and thoughtful suggestions on the rewrite. Thanks to the many women who graciously shared their stories and personal journeys with me. For their prayers, stories, and support, I am grateful to Flo Perkins, whose address has changed to heaven since the original writing of this book, Peggy Stewart, Jo Hayes, Janet Page, Melanie Hemry, Cathy Herndon, Pam Whitley, Pat Fuller, Lynn Parsley, Cynthia Morris, Cyndi Lamb Curry, Linda Leddy, Esther Heritage, Stephanie Thompson, and Maisie Bross. Thanks to Leslie Vernick for reading and advising me on one of the chapters.

Many thanks to Cindy and Chip McWilliams, who graciously allowed me to retreat to their house on the lake and complete the writing of this book.

And an extra-special thank you to my husband, Holmes, for your love and prayers during these thirty-three years as God turned my fear into faith and together we followed the great adventure.

one

Facing Our Fear

The Bible is true—and it is true!—
Fear, worrying, and anxiety actually question the trustworthiness of God.

Corrie ten Boom

Has anyone ever said to you, "You look nervous" or "You seem so afraid"? Even if you try to look really calm, there are telltale signs. You know you're experiencing fear or anxiety when . . .

- The armrest on the passenger side of your vehicle has permanent imprints from your fingers gripping it for dear life while your teen drives. Extra points if you press on invisible brakes when the car approaches another vehicle.
- Your dentist suggests you wear a mouth guard while you sleep because you are grinding your teeth.
- You are giving a speech but can't tell whether the sound you hear is the audience applauding or your knees knocking.
- The words your kids hear most from you when they go out the door are "Be careful!"
- You have a tape playing over and over in your mind, rehearsing all the "what ifs."

- You discover your nightgown is on backward and your fingernails are your favorite bedtime snack.

Perhaps your nightgown's not on backward and you aren't wearing a mouth guard yet, but you have been so anxious you couldn't catch your breath. And maybe when you're in front of an audience or in the face of a challenging situation, your hands tremble or you become nauseous. Maybe, like me, you have struggled with fear, anxiety, panic, or worry since childhood.

> Fear imprisons, faith liberates; fear paralyzes, faith empowers; fear disheartens, faith encourages; fear sickens, faith heals; fear makes useless, faith makes serviceable—and, most of all, fear puts hopelessness at the heart of life, while faith rejoices in God.
>
> *Harry Emerson Fosdick*

We live in an age of anxiety, in a world that doesn't feel safe anymore, in a time when headlines can bring us to a state of mild worry or sheer panic. A few years ago those headlines warned us of mad cow disease, Y2K, or a new computer virus. But during the past few years of terrorist attacks, anthrax incidents, child kidnappings, violence in schools, economic insecurity, the deadly SARS virus, and sniper shootings, fears have escalated. *Will my child be abducted like all the other children I've read about in the news? Is his school safe? Will there be a smallpox epidemic or chemical warfare? Will I lose my job in the economic recession? Will I come down with the West Nile virus?*

Even the use of the word *fear* has skyrocketed in the news, doubling in the 1990s, tripling since 2000. One out of four Americans will be diagnosed with an anxiety disorder at some point in their lifetime, and one out of three experienced a panic attack last year. Since September 11, 2001, our nation has been on edge, and Americans have been under a blanket of insecurity. Surveys after 9–11 showed nearly 60 percent of adults were fearful they or a family member would become the victim of a terrorist attack. For the same reason, 50 percent were afraid to open their mail.

And though the magnitude of the fears began to dissipate with time, thousands reported still having trouble sleeping and making decisions; pharmacists reported increased demands for antianxiety drugs, with 37 percent of the population reporting being worried about a chemical or biological attack. Gas masks and biohazard suits were selling as fast as duct tape and plastic sheeting. Not in a long time have we had so much to fear.

I am no stranger to fear. I know what it's like for my mother's heart to experience terror when I began hemorrhaging in the sixth month of pregnancy or when we rushed our little son to the emergency room because he couldn't breathe. Or the time four houses in our neighborhood were robbed in one week, and I was all alone until my husband returned from basic training. A loved one was diagnosed with cancer and given only a few months to live. A motorcycle hurled out of control into our lane, into our vehicle. I've known fear many times. But my fears didn't start in adulthood.

Because my mother battled anxiety, I came into this world somewhat preprogrammed for fear, and the circumstances of my life reinforced it. I was a happy, active child, verbal but cautious, with a very protective mother doing her best to keep six children safe and well (one of her sources of pride was getting us all through childhood with no broken bones). In my family, worry or fear was an instinctive response. Over and over again we heard: "Don't climb that tree; you might fall!" "I can't take you kids to the zoo; you might get eaten by one of the animals!" "Don't swim in the deep part of the pool (after we'd had swimming lessons); you might drown!"

Then a series of devastating losses reinforced to me that the world was indeed a fearful, out-of-control place. When I was eight, my father had his first major heart attack. Nine months later, my grandfather died of cancer. When I was ten, my aunt drowned in a tragic accident. And when I was eleven, my father died of his fourth heart attack in the middle of the night, leaving my mom a thirty-six-year-old, anxious single parent with six children to raise. Less than two years later, after Mom remarried, we moved, and I started a new school, one of my closest friends, just thirteen like me, died in a hunting accident at his grandpa's farm.

Any vestige of trust or faith was blown out of my life with that gun blast. In my teen years I was afraid of driving on rainy or icy streets, flying, and speaking before a group. I feared changes, feared people, and especially feared losing someone else I loved. In marriage, even more fears were introduced. Though I was never one for adventure, naturally I married a man who thrives on it. During the Vietnam War, his number one choice of service in the Air National Guard was jumping out of airplanes and then tending to the wounded, which gave me something new to worry about.

> Said the Robin to the Sparrow, "I should really like to know why these anxious human beings rush about and worry so?"
>
> Said the Sparrow to the Robin, "Friend, I think that it must be that they have no heavenly Father such as cares for you and me."
>
> *Elizabeth Cheney*

I don't know what you do when you're afraid, but one of my coping mechanisms was staying very busy, unconsciously trying to keep the darkness at bay. Sometimes people seem to avoid their fears by keeping up a frantic pace—being a supermom, superwife, church volunteer, or businessperson. Yet underneath it all, they begin to feel more and more distant from God, and they begin to see him as a taskmaster instead of a loving Father.

Some people use other means to cope with fear: They deny it, sink into depression and withdrawal, abuse alcohol and drugs, accept feeling fearful as their lot in life, or try to control things. None of these strategies truly helps us overcome our fears or brings us freedom. Instead, we can take a close look at what pushes our panic buttons, face our fears, and look to God, letting him teach us what to do when we are afraid. He can help us find new freedom from anxiety and new joy in living.

In the pages ahead I'll share with you how God turned my fears into faith in him and taught me to live life with a sense of the adventure instead of being paralyzed by anxiety. But it's not just my story. You'll also hear the stories of many women who were set free from their fears and anxieties. In the first half of the book, we'll look at the toll fear takes on us and the difference between healthy and unhealthy fears. Then I'll share overarching principles that will help you overcome any type of fear and core strategies that you can apply to many different life circumstances, things like being centered on who God is, applying God's truth, 5 Ps for overcoming panic, putting energy into prayer instead of focusing on fears, and acceptance as the doorway to peace.

In the second half, we'll look at how to overcome specific fears like fears related to your children, the fear of failure, fear of flying, fear about finances, and fears related to health problems or uncontrollable disasters. Each chapter contains true stories not only for inspiration but to illustrate the problem and the solution, strategies for overcoming fear and building a strong faith, Scriptures and quotes, and prayers for you to personalize and make your own.

The last part of the book is a small group study that you can use in a church setting, a neighborhood Bible study, or as an individual to help the principles and truths go deeper into your life.

How to Get the Most from This Book

What are the fears and anxieties that weigh you down on a regular basis? What are the situations that push your panic button? The chapters that follow can help you break free to experience greater faith, fulfillment, and intimacy with God. There are some things you can do to get the most from the journey.

Keep a notebook or journal handy. You'll need it for specific activities and applications suggested throughout the book. You can also use it to write down your thoughts about the specific fears described or memories of your own experiences that surface. Record questions and insights that arise as you read. Writing a letter to God in your notebook after reading a chapter is also helpful. Psalm 62:8 says, "Pour out your hearts to him, for God is our refuge." Besides being one of the best stress reducers, pouring out your heart on paper also helps you get in touch with what you are feeling, what God is saying to you, and how he is working in your life.

Get a package of 3x5-inch cards to use in some of the chapter applications, to make a Peace Packet, and to record verses from the Bible that are meaningful to you. Note the "Lifeline" verses in the chapters. Chosen because they relate to the specific fears each chapter discusses, they are excellent for meditating on, praying back to God, and memorizing. As you replace negative, fearful thoughts with God's promises and truth, your life will be transformed.

If you'd like to use this book for group or individual study, read the questions for discussion and reflection in the last part of the book, and look up the Scriptures for going deeper and meditating on God's Word. This section is especially designed to provide opportunities for interaction, discussion, and for applying the material to your real, walking-around, everyday life. Fear and anxiety are good issues to tackle in a group setting, and the support you can offer each other is invaluable.

My prayer is that the Lord will use the pages ahead like the bread he got from the little boy on the hill that day when there were multitudes of hungry people who needed to be fed. I offer him my heart and experience, my simple stories and words, and ask him to divide and multiply them to meet whatever need you have in this season. I pray he will bring you freedom from fear, build and strengthen your faith, and bring you into a more intimate, fulfilling relationship with him than you've ever experienced before.

two

The High Cost of Fear

Fear makes men believe the worst.

Quintus Rufus,
Alexander the Great

Margot's fear was triggered when she found out that in six days, she would be without a home because her landlord had sold the house she leased. Mary Ann's panic button was pushed when a gun was taken away from one of her daughter's classmates at school. Carol's anxiety escalated when she heard on the news that the threat level had been raised from code yellow to code orange because hospitals and schools were being targeted by terrorists. And Carrie's battle with fear began when her husband was diagnosed with Parkinson's disease.

A major ministry organization's survey of more than fifteen thousand Christians showed that fear is the number one emotional issue for women. And that was before 9-11. Maybe you don't have the fears I mentioned in chapter 1, but what are the fears and anxieties that affect you in your daily life?

Many moms worry about the health of their children. Others fear the chaotic world their kids are growing up in. Mothers of adolescents are often afraid their kids may get involved in alcohol, drugs, or the wrong crowd. One friend I know prayed the rapture would take place before her boys grew into their teen years (it didn't, but they're making it!). A big fear for many women involves the struggle to surrender control: *If I don't control things, who will? Everything will fall apart!*

Health concerns such as cancer, especially breast cancer, are prominent among things women worry about. If we don't take hormones, we may have heart disease or osteoporosis, doctors tell us; but then the new studies linking breast cancer to estrogen come out, and we're afraid to take them. We feel doomed either way. We try to eat the right foods, but then the research study of the month shows us that what we thought was good for us is now considered harmful.

> **Anxiety is a thin stream of fear trickling through the mind. If encouraged, it cuts a channel into which all other thoughts are drained.**
>
> *Arthur Somers Roche*

Some women fear success because of the role conflict it causes with their mates and their priorities as mothers. Others fear that they can't make it financially on their own if their marriages fail or their husbands are laid off. Single women tell me, "If I lose my job, I have no one to depend on" and "I'm afraid I'll lose my friends; I continually fear loneliness."

The events of the last decade, such as the Oklahoma City bombing and the attacks on the World Trade Center and Pentagon, cause us to fear the unknown, the future, and possible disasters. As the world grows more uncertain and violent, women's fears escalate. Women today have a much greater fear of random violence involving crimes such as rape, robbery, car jacking, and school shootings.

Overall, most people's greatest fears involve loss—loss of loved ones, loss of health, loss of personal safety or financial security. Experts say the most common mental health problem women face today is anxiety, and that women suffer more from fear, panic disorders, and distress than men do.

Caught in the Grip

Where does fear come from? And what is the difference between healthy and unhealthy fears? Healthy fears keep us from walking into highway traffic, motivate us to protect our kids by using child-proof caps on medicines, and make us want to lock our cars and homes, drive the speed limit, and take other intelligent precautions. Suppose a child kidnapping has been in the news. You begin to feel anxious about your own children being abducted.

Instead of obsessing over it and losing sleep because of your fears, however, you do some research and discover that statistically kidnapping is very unlikely. But you also find precautions you and your children's teachers and caretakers can implement. You equip your children to deal appropriately with strangers, and you take other steps to protect them. Your fear has led you to a better understanding of the issue and to action, and that's a good thing.

Fear is a God-given response and is one of our most basic human emotions designed to warn us to avoid or react to danger. It comes from a little almond-shaped cluster of cells in our brains, the amygdala, and causes the fight-or-flight defense mechanisms and the release of the chemicals adrenaline and noradrenaline (which make our heart race and make us shout, jump, or flee). In some ways fear is a gift to help us avoid violence or harm. It warns the child to back away from the heat of the open flame. It prompts the woman to invite a friend on a night errand to the mall after she hears a customer was robbed in the parking lot the previous week.

Fear, says Webster's Dictionary, is "an unpleasant emotional state characterized by anticipation of pain or danger." It is an inborn alarm that goes off when something's ahead that may cause pain or distress. It has two distinct parts: anxiety, which means being preoccupied with an impending threat or danger; and worry, which is the internal struggle to try to escape the danger or avoid the harmful situation.

For example, when mail was laced with deadly anthrax, people began worrying about how they could get the antibiotic Cipro (and some insisted their doctors prescribe it even though they weren't exposed to anthrax). For a period of time, many were anxious about opening their mail, afraid they might be the next victim. They avoided opening suspicious packages or envelopes with an unfamiliar return address.

Yet fear sometimes persists long after the danger is past, or a person experiences it in far bigger proportions than the situation warrants. Consider, for instance, the person who overreacted to the anthrax incidents by never going into a post office again or who avoided opening any piece of mail after that time. A fear may escalate in ways that harm, limit, or even paralyze a person—the fear turns into something they think about all the time, and they can't shake the concern. They develop headaches and insomnia, and the anxiety can grow into a panic disorder where they become afraid of the very fear itself.

While some fears have a valid source, many spring from inner motivations or fantasies that may not be grounded in reality, for example, being afraid of failing a test when you've studied hard and done well on previous tests, being arachnophobic when you haven't ever been bitten by a spider, being fearful of getting sick although you've enjoyed good health. These unhealthy and paralyzing fears are the ones we need to look at more closely.

The Effects of Fear

What a toll fear takes on our lives! It is the greatest barrier to our becoming all God has created us to be. Moreover, fear has several devastating effects.

Fear causes confusion and faulty thinking. Our brains contain more than two billion megabytes of capacity to handle the challenges and problems of daily life. But when we're preoccupied with fear, thoughts become tangled and logical thinking can actually be blocked. Chronically anxious people complain they can't concentrate and are easily distracted from daily chores and tasks.

Fear saps our energy. All of us have a certain supply of emotional and physical energy called "calendar energy," or the amount of inner resources (including emotional energy and physical strength) we have in a twenty-four-hour period to deal with life. If we use it up being anxious and fearful, we can literally run out of gas and burn out. I don't know about you, but I need all the energy I can muster to deal with what's on my plate each day.

Fear limits our potential. God has given each of us gifts and talents he wants us to use, but fear keeps our talents in the closet. Fear causes us to avoid new situations and miss taking advantage of opportunities to develop and utilize our gifts. "All of us have reservoirs of full potential," said Swiss psychiatrist Paul Tournier, "but the road that leads to those reservoirs is guarded by the dragon of fear."[1] Fear can sideline you from serving others and stunt your fruitfulness, especially when what God is calling you to do involves taking a risk or leaving your comfort zone.

> **God does not want us to fear because fear prevents us from receiving and doing all He has planned for us. He loves and wants to bless us and has provided ways for us not to fear.**
>
> Joyce Meyer, Help Me, I'm Afraid

Fear harms relationships. Commonsense caution is a good thing, but fear causes us to overprotect or try to control our children and teenagers. If we fear rejection, we tend to wear a mask, avoid heart-to-heart communication with people, and avoid commitments, thus sabotaging close relationships and especially marriages.

Fear sets us up for failure. "I was afraid that was going to happen!" said a mother of a teenage driver who had just had his first accident. Fear creates what we fear; it has a magnetism that attracts or quickens the approach of the feared event. As Job said, "What I fear comes upon me, and what I dread befalls me" (Job 3:25 NASB). For example, if you're afraid of a dog biting you, you increase the possibility of being bitten. If you focus on your fear of gaining weight, diet experts say you may be setting yourself up for extra poundage.

Fear robs us of faith. Just like a seesaw, fear and faith rise and fall proportionately. When one increases, the other decreases. Second Timothy 1:7 says that God has not given us a spirit of fear but of power and love and a sound, strong mind. But when fear robs you of faith, then power, strength, and a loving attitude go out the door also.

Fear focuses us on the wrong things. Sometimes we fear the things we shouldn't and don't fear the things we should. I recently read about a man who is petrified of riding on roller coasters but doesn't wear a seat belt in the car and drives his motorcycle at 165 mph without a helmet. Millions of us fear electromagnetic or nuclear radiation but don't worry about spending hours in the sun absorbing statistically more dangerous, cancer-causing ultraviolet radiation. They routinely make calls on their cell phones while cruising on the highway, even though studies show that drivers using cell phones cause as many wrecks as drivers under the influence of alcohol.

> Anxiety has its use, stimulating us to seek with keener longing for that security where peace is complete and unassailable.
>
> *St. Augustine*

Fear steals our joy. If you're a visual person with an active imagination, you may turn your anxieties into mental motion pictures that play on the movie screen of your mind. Or you may replay your mental tape recorder with negative messages and "what ifs." In either case, it's hard to be happy and anxious at the same time. Since the joy of the Lord is your strength (Neh. 8:10), if your joy is drained away by fear and anxiety about tomorrow, it empties you of the strength you need for today.

All of the above are great reasons not to stuff our fears or deny our fears but to deal with them head-on and break free.

What Does God Say about Fear?

In the midst of our anxious, fear-filled world, God tells us an amazing thing: *Don't fear.* Over and over throughout Scripture, over 366 times, God tells us not to be anxious, afraid, worried, or terrified. The One who knows the end from the beginning knows every fear that men and women will struggle with. Yes, the stakes are up and the fearsome things in our world seem to multiply. And yet, no matter what we have to face, whether our fears are legitimate or are produced by an overactive imagination, God's message doesn't change:

> But now, O Israel, the LORD who created you says: "Do not be afraid, for I have ransomed you. I have called you by name; you are mine. When you go through deep waters and great trouble, I will be with you. When you go through rivers of difficulty, you will not drown! When you walk through the fire of oppression, you will not be burned up; the flames will not consume you . . . For I am the LORD, your God, the Holy One of Israel, your Savior . . . You are precious to me. You are honored, and I love you. Do not be afraid, for I am with you."
>
> Isaiah 43:1–5 NLT

> Have I not commanded you? Be strong and courageous! Do not tremble or be dismayed, for the LORD your God is with you wherever you go.
>
> Joshua 1:9 NASB

> Peace I leave with you; My peace I give to you; not as the world gives, do I give to you. Let not your heart be troubled, nor let it be fearful.
>
> John 14:27 NASB

> Do not fear, for I am with you;
> Do not anxiously look about you, for I am your God.
> I will strengthen you, surely I will help you.
> Surely I will uphold you with My righteous right hand.
>
> Isaiah 41:10 NASB

Since God tells us not to fear, he must have some secrets for us. In the next chapter we will look at the first and most important key to overcoming fear: focusing on the God who can calm our hearts, instead of focusing on our problems, our fears, or the "what ifs."

three

Centered on the Greatness of God

When we are lost in the greatness of God, we realize that there is no physical, emotional, or social loss so great that God cannot bring good out of it and compensate us in the next life.

Gary Thomas

It was the dead of winter, and we were living in Yarmouth, Maine. Discouragement was wrapping itself around my neck like ivy twining around a house—ivy so thick that if left untamed, it could cover the brick and windows and shut out the light. A cold blanket of fear covered me, draining me of energy. I felt tired, anxious, and burdened.

My husband was out of work and depressed. Day after day he interviewed for jobs and was rejected. Our savings long gone, I was afraid we couldn't pay the mounting bills. Some days I was afraid Holmes was going to give up; he seemed to have lost hope in life. We were both afraid we'd never have the money to return to our hometown in Oklahoma.

The long-term effects of stress and worry were taking their toll. Normally optimistic and able to encourage my somewhat melancholy spouse, I was struggling. I kept reading my Bible and talking to God in this wilderness season, but my eyes kept landing on the worrisome circumstances. I poured out my heart to him but heard no answers.

Finally one evening I shared with the people in our Monday night Bible study group how trying a time it was for us. Although they prayed for us, things only got worse financially and my anxiety grew. A few weeks later one of the women took me aside and said, "Cheri, no matter how hard things are, you must praise and thank God in the midst of your circumstances. Focus on him, not your trouble. That's not a message from me but from my missionary friend Anne. She wants you to know she's praying for you."

> When my eyes are on the Lord, He gives me a spirit of calmness—a strong, solid trust and dependency that rests in Him alone. Because He is my refuge, I can live freely and fearlessly, knowing that God is always in control.
>
> *Rebecca Barlow Jordan*

Are you kidding? I wanted to say. *Thank and praise God when I feel so afraid and down about things?* I'd heard Linda talk about this elderly missionary woman who had served in China before World War II and had survived prison camp, but I had never met her. I knew she was right, though, and I knew it was what the Bible said too, but it was a hard message to hear in that particular moment. *I always thought you wanted genuine not fake praise, Lord, and I want to be real with you. How can I rejoice in you and not drown in the circumstances we're in?*

I pondered that question all week, trying to force myself to praise God, but I failed miserably. I wanted to be faithful in this, but I felt overwhelmed and I was drained from trying to bolster my depressed husband. Falling deeper into discouragement and as anxious as ever, I asked Linda the next week if I could go with her on her weekly trip to see Anne. I thought if anyone could shed some light on my problems, this wise missionary could.

That bitterly cold December day, we visited Anne and her Scottish nurse, Netta, at their apartment on the top of the hill. As we walked in, I saw a white-haired woman in a burgundy sweater sitting in a recliner, legs propped up and covered with a small green blanket. Print-patterned house shoes peeked out from the blanket.

Above the old missionary hung a plaque with the words, "Let us exalt the Lord together." Another said, "Jesus First." A humidifier hummed. After taking our coats, Netta went with Linda into the other room to wrap Christmas packages to mail to missionaries the two elderly women supported. Although they had very little financially, they regularly gave to ministries and missionaries and were remembering each with a Scripture calendar that year.

Trust God

Anne was almost totally blind, but her spiritual eyesight blew me away. She spoke with effort but with a quiet authority, asking me all about our situation. She seemed to have an understanding of my life far beyond what I shared, and after listening, she offered some insights. "For your children's and your husband's sakes, you must praise and thank God and show in your countenance your faith in him. For she who trusts him finds him wholly true.

"Trust and thank God in all things," she continued. "Praise him even if tears are running down your cheeks."

I nodded but grimaced inside, thinking this sounded impossible. "But how?" I asked. "I want so much to praise and thank God, and I've tried, but it's so hard when I'm worried and depressed."

"By trusting God implicitly," she added. "You can't depend on your feelings; they are Satan's playground. Ask for God's grace to praise him and he'll give it to you."

A few moments later, Linda and Netta came in with our coats and began to bundle Anne up to leave for the restaurant. As painstakingly slow and difficult as it was with her diabetic condition and leg problems, Anne needed to get out once a day and walk with her walker, so back into the cold we went. One of us walked on each side of the elderly woman, our arm under hers.

A Story of God's Faithfulness

Over our salads and bowls of soup, I asked about Anne's experiences as a missionary in China. She shared about the day she was leaving Shanghai for furlough in her beloved Scotland. After nine years of service with the China Inland Mission, she couldn't wait to see her family and friends and was overdue for a respite. She and the other missionaries had packed their belongings and were stepping out of the mission house to get on the boat when Anne heard a clamor outside. As she watched through the window, she saw Japanese soldiers goose-stepping in unison down the street, knees almost up to their noses. The Lord spoke to her heart, "Anne, come aside. I want to talk to you."

Reminding her of his care and provision during many adventures and close calls, he told her she was not going home but would be a prisoner of the Japanese. He didn't tell her how long, but she distinctly heard, "I'll be with you." A precious, very real sense of God's nearness and peace filled her as he spoke. Then, "Do you have any prayer requests to make, Anne?" he asked.

Although she'd never given her teeth a thought, the Spirit nudged Anne to pray that her teeth would be preserved and not one of them fall out. So out of obedience more than vanity, she asked this of God.

Moments later she and the other English and American missionaries were taken prisoner and marched to a Japanese prison camp. There she spent three and a half years in near starvation, dreadful cold in winter, scorching heat in summer. Cruelty, rats, disease, and death were all around her. There were no Bibles, so she had to rely on all the verses she had committed to memory.

She chuckled as she told me about the rat she had found up her sleeve in the middle of the night and the "Rat Patrol" she headed up after that to try to make the barracks a safer place for the other women and children. She shared about God's constant presence, the people who came to know Christ, how she gave him every burden, worry, and fear and saw him work time after time. Anne seemed to possess this quiet assurance that she could absolutely trust God because he was worthy. She could have been overwhelmed by fear or consumed by despair until she couldn't minister at all, but she didn't focus on the "what ifs": *What if I don't survive? What if my health breaks? What if we're not rescued?*

Instead, she fixed her eyes on Jesus and his promise that he would never leave, fail, or forsake her (Heb. 13:5–6). He hadn't failed her yet, and she knew she could count on him for tomorrow. So instead of fearing, she used her energies to serve God, to proclaim Christ, and to love those around her.

Story after story she related about God's provision in the prison camp. I sat there spellbound, marveling at the mercy and faithfulness of the God she and I serve. And as I listened, my trials came into perspective in the light of her experiences.

> Surrender to the Lord means turning around one hundred and eighty degrees—that means a renewed person and renewed vision. . . . We are not ready for the battle until we have seen the Lord, for Jesus is the answer to all problems.
>
> *Corrie ten Boom,* Reflections of His Glory

Anne was released after World War II ended. And though she was in poor health, every tooth was preserved! But other losses awaited her. Her mother had died while she was in prison camp. And now, although she was dealing with the day-to-day trials of aging—her vision was failing and she had already suffered several surgeries—she encouraged my friend and me: "Trust. Cast all your cares and fears on him. No matter what's on your mind, roll it onto his shoulders and rest under his wing."

On the way home, my thoughts were filled with Anne's stories and the truth she had shared. It was as if she had pulled my eyes and hands off my problems and fixed them on the Lord and his faithfulness. Her words came back to me: "Don't lean on your own understanding. Don't trust what you see or feel or think; trust God and his Word. He's faithful even when we're not."

I prayed silently, "Lord, I want to focus on you and praise you right in the middle of our circumstances and I ask for your grace to help me do that."

The Turnaround

That night the checking account balance hadn't changed. My husband still didn't have a job and was just as withdrawn and depressed as usual, but something new was engaging my thoughts. The next few days, in the early hours before the kids got up, I searched the Bible, especially the Psalms, for words to praise God, to center my thoughts on him. All the feelings of worry and anxiety were still lurking around, trying to drag me down, but I knelt and used Scripture verses to adore the Lord. This time I didn't wait until I felt better to praise him.

As I praised God, that deep heaviness began to lift and with it my anxiety about our stack of unpaid bills. It was as if dark glasses were removed and I saw what I'd never seen before: that no matter how difficult our situation was and even if nothing external changed, I could praise and thank God because the trial would only draw me into a closer relationship with him.

Like a trickle from a frozen creek in the spring, that icy fear within me began to thaw little by little, and thanksgiving bubbled up. Slowly at first, my perspective began to change. I wasn't a prisoner of my feelings but could trust and enjoy God for the first time in a long time—no list of complaints or requests. I thanked him for the inner work he was doing in us, for our health, our children, our marriage that was still together—even the fact that it was strained had drawn me closer to him. I thanked him for the plan he had for us even though we didn't see it, and even for our financial losses because they reminded me that material things were temporary but our eternal treasures in Christ would last forever.

Lost in the Greatness of God

How could Anne face what she did and not be overcome by fear or despair? She was centered on God, lost in his greatness, and focused on his faithfulness, love, and character. Whatever fear you have—whether related to finances, children, disasters, health, or a difficult situation you are facing—focusing on the Lord is a key to overcoming fear when life gets scary.

"Keep looking in the right direction in everything you do—that is so important. Keep looking up and kneeling down," said Corrie ten Boom, another woman who overcame the horrors of a concentration camp and took the message of Christ's love and forgiveness around the world following her release. One day she met a missionary who was desperate because Christians were continually being killed near her home.

"Look down on the storms and terrible events around us, down from on high," Corrie told her, "from the heavenly realms where Jesus' victory is the greatest reality. This is only possible by the Holy Spirit." She told the woman how she and her sister Betsie were walking around the German prison grounds at 4:30 A.M. one morning when God performed a miracle. Betsie would say something, Corrie would say something—then the Lord would speak and they both heard him at the same time:

> I cannot explain it, but it was wonderful. We saw then that even though everything was terrible, we could rely on the fact that God did not have any problems, only plans. There is never panic in heaven! You can only hold on to that reality through faith because it seemed then as it often seems now, as if the devil is the victor. But God is faithful, and His plans never fail! He knows the future! He knows the way.[1]

That vision of God's greatness empowered Corrie not to fear and not to panic even though she faced overwhelming loss, pain, and danger. It sustained and strengthened her when she traveled the world in her sixties and seventies to share the message God gave her. Just as God was there for Anne, Corrie, and countless believers throughout history, he will be our stability in an unstable world. He is our unchangeable certainty when everything around us is changing. And there is no more secure, safe place than in the center of his will and purpose for our lives.

Having our eyes on the Lord in this way is vital—David experienced it and described it throughout the Psalms. No matter how badly he hurt or what he feared, he turned his focus to God and proclaimed who God was. Though he was surrounded by a host of enemies time after time, he could say, "The LORD is my light and my salvation. Whom shall I fear? The LORD is the strength of my life; of whom shall I be afraid?" (Ps. 27:1). Paul too said we must fix our eyes on Jesus and press on to know him (Phil. 3).

> The remarkable thing about fearing God is that when you fear God you fear nothing else, whereas if you do not fear God you fear everything else.
>
> *Oswald Chambers*

When we look to God and focus on him instead of our problems and fears, we gain his perspective. Our fears begin to melt away as the things of this world grow strangely dim in the light of his glory and grace. It doesn't mean we won't go through difficult times or experience pain. But we begin to know and believe that we can trust him in the midst of our circumstances, for he is trustworthy.

From Fear to Faith

Our faith as believers isn't just a passport to heaven; eternal life doesn't just start when we die. It begins here on earth as we make him the center of our lives. Jesus talked about the importance of knowing God and focusing on him in John 17:3: "This is eternal life: that they may know you, the only true God, and Jesus Christ, whom you have sent." How can we move from fear to developing this kind of faith? How can we stop being preoccupied by our fears and problems and get lost in the greatness of God?

Cultivate a lifestyle of praise. Why did Anne encourage me to praise and thank God even when I didn't feel like it? Because praise gets our eyes off the mountains and on the Mountain Mover and has many other benefits as well. We're not talking about praise as just a few worship songs sung at the beginning of a service but a Godward focus in the midst of whatever we're facing. As Ruth Myers, a missionary with the Navigators since 1972, says, it's realizing "God uses tough situations to draw you nearer to Him and to enrich your praise."[2]

This doesn't mean denying your real feelings, she adds. You may be experiencing intense feelings of fear or sorrow. It's expressing your distressing emotions (including despair, guilt, fear, or anger) to God, yet choosing to keep proclaiming who God is and turning to him in spite of how things look to you— and not postponing this until you feel better. It's moving toward the Lord in your distress instead of away from him and developing a faith that goes beyond your feelings.

At first you may start to thank God with little trickles as I did, but if you persist, even in the darkest of places, you will find those trickles of faith will turn into a fountain. As you do, your attitude can turn from anxiety to trust. You may even begin to see your situation differently: "Praise can heighten your awareness that distressing circumstances are God's blessings in disguise. Your trials rip away the flimsy fabric of your self-sufficiency. This makes room for God's Spirit to weave into your life a true and solid confidence—the kind of confidence that Paul expressed in Philippians 4:13: 'I can do all things through Christ who strengthens me'" (NKJV).[3]

When we focus on God and proclaim who he is, we begin to see clearly who is in control. Our focus is drawn from the complexity of the problem to the adequacy of God's infinite resources.[4]

Fear God instead of people or circumstances. The Bible tells us to exchange a fear of situations or persons for a fear of God. A holy, healthy fear comes out of reverence, wonder, and awe of the God who created us, knew us before we were even born, and loves us. David demonstrated the fear of God many times. When he faced formidable enemies, "he understood that he could not simply will his fears away. The person (or persons) he feared had to be displaced by something bigger: fear of the Lord and trust in His provision," says Dave Shive.[5]

Whereas fear of circumstances directs us to a horizontal focus and can paralyze us, throw us into a pity party, or consume us with worry, fear of God—that wonder and respect of who he is—

leads us to a vertical focus and propels us to worship him and enjoy life and relationships on the horizontal level. I'm not speaking of an unhealthy fear of God, one that causes us to shrink from him because we think he'll smack us for doing the wrong thing or to avoid turning our lives over to him completely because we don't trust what he'll do with us.

In contrast, a healthy fear and reverence of the Lord, the Bible tells us, is clean; it prolongs life and is the beginning of wisdom (see Pss. 19:9; 111:10). The benefits of having a worshipful wonder of God are terrific. If we know the incredible power of the One who holds the future, then we don't have to fear the future even if it looks uncertain, for he is with us (Ps. 23:4).

> Relinquishment of burdens and fears begins where adoration and worship of God become the occupation of the soul.
>
> *Frances J. Roberts*

Know his name. I'm convinced that our puny or incorrect perspective of God is the root of many of our fears. And I know when I let fear—over finances, the future, my health, or anything else—sap my strength, it is because I have forgotten how awesome, how able, how loving and faithful God truly is.

"Those who know your name will trust in you, for you, LORD, have never forsaken those who seek you," says Psalm 9:10. Our faith in God develops as we know his names. As I have lived with my husband, Holmes, for thirty-three years, I have come to know and experience him in the different aspects of his nature as my companion, lover, best friend, prayer partner, generous giver, faithful father of our children (and now also grandfather), builder of beautiful homes, and much more. In a similar way, we know God in experiencing different aspects of his character and person. In the Bible these different ways he revealed himself are sometimes known as "His Names."

I have found that when I become anxious or fearful about things, one of the best antidotes is to refocus on God by meditating on his names, that he is Elohim, Creator of the whole universe, yet he cares about me and my family. That he is Jehovah

Nissi, the Lord My Banner, and his banner over me is love. One of God's names is Emmanuel, God with Us—not at a distance but nearer than our breath, constantly working in our lives. His name is Jehovah Rapha, the Lord Our Healer, who specializes in healing relationships and broken hearts and renewing our weary spirits. In reminding myself of who God is and bringing him more clearly into focus, my heart becomes centered on God and finds courage to trust him once again.

When I understand God's names, my heart begins to trust him. And coming to him with my needs or the needs of others in prayer becomes a whole different matter than just hoping he might help me. It's knowing whom we are addressing, confident that we aren't asking anything outside of who God is. For example, we can trust that when we pray to Jehovah Jireh, the Lord Our Provider, he sees our needs and delights to provide for them because that is who he is. Just as he provided in the past, he'll provide in the future. That is who he is, and it's an essential part of his nature that he wants us to experience. The more we know his nature through his names, the more our faith grows, and the more our fears are overcome.

> When I am with God
> My fear is gone
> In the great quiet of God.
> My troubles are as the
>   pebbles on the road,
> My joys are like the
>   everlasting hills.
>
> *Walter Rauschenbusch*

The Lifeline of God's Word

Praying Scripture is one of the most powerful things we can do to dissolve our fears and to grow in our relationship with the Lord. In the next chapter, we're going to delve into focusing on God's Word, praying Scripture, and exchanging the lies for the truth. And in each chapter there will be verses for you to pray back to God. To begin, take one of the following verses and let the prayer below it be a springboard for your own communication with God:

O magnify the LORD with me,
And let us exalt His name together.
I sought the LORD, and He answered me,
And delivered me from all my fears.
They looked to Him and were radiant,
And their faces will never be ashamed.

Psalm 34:3–5 NASB

Lord, I want to magnify you and exalt your name. I am seeking you and asking that you would deliver me from all my fears. As I look to you, I thank and praise you that you have promised I will be radiant and my face shall never be ashamed.

Why are you in despair, O my soul?
And why have you become disturbed within me?
Hope in God, for I shall again praise Him
For the help of His presence.

Psalm 42:5 NASB

Praise him in his Temple,
and in the heavens he made with mighty power.
Praise him for his mighty works.
Praise his unequaled greatness . . .
Let everything alive give praises to the Lord!
You praise him!

Psalm 150:1–2, 6 TLB

Father, I admit that I've been in despair and fear, my heart disturbed within me. I want to hope in you, for with the help of your presence and your Spirit, I will again praise you! I praise you for your mighty power and mighty works!

four

Focusing on the Truth

All the promises in the Bible become your property. But you
have to find your way around in that world of riches. You
have to find out how rich you are.

Corrie ten Boom

When Cathy's daughter Susan was going blind, she agonized
over what was happening. Susan had a car she couldn't
drive; her boyfriend dropped her suddenly; and her college roommate moved out the week before finals without saying a word. The family had prayed with and for Susan, trusting
God with the situation. But their struggles continued with a
vengeance as her blindness progressed rapidly that summer.

As a mother, Cathy had never gone through such a painful
and fear-producing experience. She would sleep at night but upon
awakening, tears would already be streaming from her eyes. Anx-

ious thoughts would rush in. *Will Susan be able to finish college? What about her dreams? What about marriage and the future?* She would cry and then wash her face and pick up her Bible. "God, I've taught in Sunday school for years that you are my comfort and hope; I need your comfort just now." As she read, verse after verse soothed her aching heart. They strengthened her to face the day and minister to her hurting daughter, her family, and the women in her Sunday school class.

Each morning as Cathy read the Bible, God would give her a different verse about his hope, his security, and his comfort. She learned she must let Christ set her heart mood for the day from his Word. She learned she must focus on what God said instead of what she felt. If she looked at worrisome circumstances or why something happened, she would spiral down to depression and fear.

How firm a foundation, ye saints of the Lord,

Is laid for your faith in His excellent Word!

What more can He say than to you He hath said,

To you who for refuge to Jesus has fled?

"How Firm a Foundation" words from "K" in Rippon's Selection, 1787

One morning when she read Isaiah 26:3, "He will keep in perfect peace all those who trust in him, whose thoughts turn often to the Lord" (TLB), Cathy had an idea: She would write these verses down to carry with her everywhere she went and focus her mind on them throughout the day. As she did this, she found not only did it keep her from dwelling on the dismal "what ifs," but her thoughts were gradually transformed from worry and sadness to a confident sense of peace.

Charles Stanley once said, "The most valuable item you can own in the time of trouble is a Bible." Cathy found hers indispensable. The Word of God was alive and powerful as she learned not to keep her attention riveted on a constant rehearsal of what had happened to her daughter or why—that thought pattern would make her easy prey for Satan. Instead she focused on God's truth. Day by day using her "Peace Packet," as her collection of Bible verses in a small Ziplock bag came to be known, she focused on Christ and his promises.

Verses like, "I, the Lord, will be with you and see you through" (Jer. 1:8 TLB) and "Jehovah himself is caring for you" dispelled fear. Psalm 112:6–9 became a passage that strengthened her faith:

> Such a man [woman] will not be overthrown by evil circumstances. God's constant care of her will make a deep impression on all who see it. She does not fear bad news, nor live in dread of what may happen. For she is settled in her mind that Jehovah will take care of her. That is why she is not afraid, but can calmly face her foes.
>
> TLB

As the summer went by, Cathy began to type these verses on cards for women in her class going through their own trials. As they noticed what peace, comfort, and strength came from her collection, Cathy's Peace Packet grew—and so did the demand for it. The little Peace Packet that came out of one family's grief has been used to help many others: a man whose wife was critically ill, a young woman whose husband left her and their two children, a missionary in harm's way in South America, a family in the emergency room awaiting word on their teenager who'd been in an auto accident.

> Faith is like radar that sees through the fog—The reality of things at a distance that the human eye cannot see.
>
> *Corrie ten Boom*

Although Susan's vision did continue to deteriorate, she finished college, even traveling to Finland on a student exchange program. She pursued many of her dreams and married. She, her husband, and son run a horse ranch in a western state, and God has truly done more than she could have asked, thought, or imagined. It doesn't mean this one experience was the end of the family's suffering or that they always respond in faith in every circumstance. But over and over they see that these promises are as fresh and real and glorious to them today as they were in their dark times over twenty years ago. The same is true for the hundreds of men and women who have also been encouraged by God's Word through Cathy's Peace Packet.

Building a Faith That Overcomes Our Fears

How can we build a faith that will overcome our fears? God speaks to us clearly on how faith is developed: "So faith comes from hearing, and hearing by the word of Christ" (Rom. 10:17 NASB). As Edith Schaeffer wrote:

> It is the Word of God, which is truth being unfolded (via) a succession of meaningful words in human language. The Word of God is the Bible. What makes it different is that it is what God has revealed to man, and is therefore true truth . . . there is a trustworthy, perfectly just and holy Person verbalizing something that can be depended upon.[1]

One of God's main strategies for us to overcome our fear, to stand firm, and to have a steadfast heart in the midst of difficult times is to protect ourselves with the armor he has provided and described in Ephesians 6:

> Use every piece of God's armor to resist the enemy in the time of evil, so that after the battle you will still be standing firm. Stand your ground, putting on the sturdy belt of truth and the body armor of God's righteousness. For shoes, put on the peace that comes from the Good News, so that you will be fully prepared. In every battle you will need faith as your shield to stop the fiery arrows aimed at you by Satan. Put on salvation as your helmet, and take the sword of the Spirit, which is the word of God.
>
> Ephesians 6:13–17 NLT

This spiritual armor is crucial for believers, both young and old. In every battle we need to put on the belt of truth as we read and meditate on God's Word and fill our minds with his truth.

Using the offensive weapon called the "Sword of the Lord," which is the Word of God, we speak, proclaim, and pray the Scriptures, all the while holding up the "Shield of Faith" that deflects the fear bombs and flaming darts from Satan. God has given us his Word as a resource for prayer and for life and for every spiritual battle we face, especially as we seek to overcome fear.

Why all this battle talk? Because we are in a battle, and fear isn't from God. He doesn't give us a spirit of fear but just the opposite: power, love, and a sound, strong mind (2 Tim. 1:7). And as Rick Joyner wrote,

> The real battle that we are fighting is against fear. . . . The devil uses fear to control people in the way that the Lord uses faith. When we begin to recognize fear itself as the work of the devil, we begin to recognize the true nature of the enemy and his intentions. . . . We submit to God by living by faith, and we resist the devil by refusing to let his fears control us in place of our faith in God.[2]

Even in the worst of situations and dangers, God's Word can steady and strengthen our hearts so we can experience calmness instead of hysterics.

The morning of September 11, 2001, began like any other for Cathy and Billy Boyd. An executive chef for a law firm on the 57th floor of the World Trade Center's North Tower, Billy left for work at 5 A.M., long before Cathy got their three children up for school. After the usual wake-up calls, breakfast, and search for socks and shoes, she hustled all three kids out the door and dropped them off at school. On her way back home, Cathy turned on the radio and heard about a fire on the top of the North Tower. Running into their apartment, Cathy flipped on the television and gasped at the sight of both towers ablaze.

Cathy fumbled for the phone and called Billy. The line was dead. Fear taunted her as spellbound, she watched the towers burn. *Terrorist attack.* The words exploded her world as surely as those planes exploded into the Twin Towers. *Billy!* Chaos reigned on the news . . . and then the television screen went black. *The antennas are on top of the towers!*

Cathy raced to a neighbor's house where they had cable. Billy had only been transferred to the towers three weeks before. Three weeks! Only days before, he'd said, "Cathy, the view of Manhattan is spectacular! On Saturday I'll bring you and the kids to see the city from the Twin Towers." Now they would never see that view—but would they ever see Billy again?

Suddenly, the first tower collapsed in a maelstrom of smoke, fire, and ashes, bodies hurtling out of windows, papers and debris flying, newsmen yelling. As the horrific scenes played across the screen, Cathy's neighbor shrieked and sobbed uncontrollably. For Cathy, time stood still. Strangely, she remembered the Scripture she'd studied the night before in Psalm 57:1: "Have mercy on me, O God, have mercy on me, for in you my soul takes refuge. I will take refuge in the shadow of your wings until the disaster has passed."

> Oh, that we would turn eye and heart from everything else and fix them upon this God who hears prayer until the magnificence of His promises and His power and His purpose of love overwhelmed us!
>
> *Andrew Murray*

"Lord," she whispered, "if Billy is in that building, he is safe in your hands." A strange calm and strength wrapped themselves around Cathy like a mother's love. God was sovereign, she knew that. No matter what happened, he would be with them. *Don't worry, he's safe,* the Spirit whispered.

Cathy's neighbor shook her. "What's wrong with you? Your husband is in that building! Why aren't you hysterical?" Cathy comforted her friend. How could she tell her that God, like a referee in a game gone sour, had yelled, "Safe!" over Billy? Cathy knew without a doubt that Billy was safe—either safe with God in heaven or safely on his way home. But he was safe under the shadow of the Almighty, in the secret place of God.

On the 57th floor of the North Tower, Billy Boyd had one thing on his mind that morning—breakfast preparations. Suddenly he felt as though a sledgehammer hit his ear. No one on that floor got the word that a terrorist had just flown an airplane into the tower a few floors above them. But *something* violent had happened. Billy climbed the stairs to the 59th floor only to discover his boss had evacuated the building. Back downstairs, Billy searched out every employee and told them to leave. Billy turned off the stove and refrigerator, and cleaned up while accounting for each and every person as they left. Finally, he started the journey down fifty-seven flights of stairs—a trip that took forty-five minutes. Reaching the ground floor, Billy ran outside and turned back in time to see the building fall.

> Just as saving faith comes through hearing the gospel, so also the faith to trust God in adversity comes through the Word of God alone. . . . Only from the Scriptures, applied to our hearts by the Holy Spirit, do we receive the grace to trust God when we are afraid.
>
> *Jerry Bridges,* Discipleship Journal

It wasn't until Cathy's cell phone rang with the message that Billy had escaped unharmed that she wept—for joy. What was it that kept Cathy from being terrified when everyone and everything around her was in hysterics and chaos? Her stability came from God's Word. It was her source of strength and hope, not only for that disaster but for all the things to come in their future.

It's important also to note that all of the pieces of armor described in Ephesians 6 describe Jesus Christ. He is the "author and finisher" of our faith (Heb. 12:2 KJV). He is the security of our salvation, and we are clothed in his righteousness (Isa. 61:10). He is the Living Word, and keeping our minds set on him unravels Satan's deceptions. He is our peace (Eph. 2:14), and as we focus on him, we don't need to fear the enemy or anything else.

Breaking Free

Every time we open our Bibles, we encounter the Living Word, Scriptures that are God-breathed truths meant to break us free from fear and anything else that would hold us in bondage (John 8:32). God's truth brings us out of old thought patterns of anxiety and helps us fight the good fight. We certainly can't fight fear in our own strength; we can't wish it away or hope it will go away if we think positive thoughts! We must use the "weapons of our warfare" that God has provided and know that they are spiritual weapons "divinely powerful for the destruction of fortresses" (2 Cor. 10:4 NASB)—no matter how deep those strongholds are.

Grace's world changed at age eight when she was sexually assaulted by two distant relatives at a family reunion. Threatened with harm to herself and her family, she kept silent, and the emotional devastation continued into her adult life. Fear was the dominant emotion that caused her to be withdrawn and distrustful of God, men, her body, and even herself. She eventually surrendered all hope of knowing freedom again.

Yet she continued to pursue a relationship with God and break through the walls she felt. One morning she was reading in John 11 of Lazarus's resurrection. Jesus called to Lazarus to *come out.* Then he told observers to take off Lazarus's grave clothes (vv. 43–44). In that moment, God spoke to her heart: "Grace, *come out.* Let others take off your grave clothes. Be free." She wept that morning as she knew that God was asking her to trust others to help her. She told her best friend what had happened, and they wept together. Her friend's compassion freed her to experience God's love and acceptance and allow others into her life.

Realizing how bound she was, she asked God to send someone to help her take steps toward freedom. Soon after, she met a lay counselor at church. As she shared her life story, he began to lead Grace through Romans and Psalm 18. He taught her biblical truth about her position in Christ and the power of the cross in daily living. God's Word became a light in her darkness as she learned to stand on its authority.

One by one, she confronted the lies she had believed about God, herself, and others with biblical truth and started facing her fears and seeing changes. Although she knew nights would be scary, she decided she could live alone. She could travel alone for business if necessary and be out after dark. She didn't have to use being overweight as her armor anymore. She could trust people's intentions toward her, reclaim her voice, and stop being a people pleaser.

John 10:10 says, "The thief comes only to steal and kill and destroy," but Jesus came that we "may have life, and have it to the full." Fear had stolen years of Grace's life, but God's promises gave her the courage to wage war against it. Finding a counselor and asking others to pray for her helped her come to a new level of freedom. Grace still struggles with fear and controlling her weight, but she is resolved not to allow fear to be a stronghold. It takes effort on her part to choose, believe, and live out of biblical truth. But even when she struggles, she is confident that:

> The LORD is my rock, my fortress and my deliverer; my God is my rock, in whom I take refuge. He is my shield and the horn of my salvation, my stronghold.
>
> Psalm 18:2

With such a God and such powerful truth, fear cannot overcome her.[3]

As Grace experienced, fear is often accompanied by the lies of the enemy, distorted beliefs, and even irrational thinking. It is essential to replace the fearful thoughts and ideas with biblical truth, as Grace learned to do.

For example, if you are suddenly diagnosed with an illness and a wave of fear and anxiety floods your mind, it is vital to focus on the Word. Replace thoughts like you'll never be able to support yourself or your kids again because of your limitations, you're so weak you don't know how you'll cope, or your illness has slipped by God's watchful care with the truth:

- God will supply all you need (Phil. 4:19), and regardless of your health issues, you are strong in him (Joel 3:10). He has given you all you need for life and godliness (2 Peter 1:3).
- He is your Great Physician, Jehovah Rapha, the Lord Our Healer, and is well able to take care of your physical needs (Exod. 15).

- You belong to Christ (1 Cor. 3:23) and nothing happens to you apart from his affectionate, watchful care (1 Peter 5:7 AMP).

As you displace the lies and fears with God's Word, you will be filled with faith and a new confidence and hope in the Lord. That's why as we address some specific fears in the chapters ahead, I will share the truths from God's Word that relate to those fears.

From Fear to Faith

We need a bridge to move from operating in fear and anxiety to living each day in faith, and God provided that bridge in his Word. The Bible is essential to our life, our health both emotionally and spiritually, and our freedom from fear. Here are some ways to apply the truths of God's Word to your life:

Face the fear. What are you afraid of? What concerns have you caught in the grip of fear? Articulate what you are afraid of and be specific. Rather than just saying, "I'm anxious," say, "I'm afraid of _____, and _____, and _____." You may need the help of a counselor or pastor to really get insight into what is pushing your panic button. Once you admit instead of deny what you are most afraid of, the light can begin to shine there, roots can begin to be revealed, and recovery can begin to take place. First confess these fears to God and then to a trusted friend or counselor.

Stand on the promises. Once you've begun to face your fears and confess them to God, ask what lies you are believing. Release these lies and replace them with God's truth. Cathy and Grace learned to stand on God's truth and his promises, which enabled them to build a strong faith and overcome fear. Psalm 91:4 says, "His faithful promises are your armor and protection" (NLT).

A faith based on God's precious promises is indestructible and irresistible, enabling us to trust him in the dark, even in the most vulnerable places and greatest difficulties. That's why it's so important to renew your mind day by day with God's Word (Rom. 12:2) and look for specific truths to replace the lies you have previously believed.

A truth like "He Who fills me with His dynamic power has made me able to cope with any situation" (Phil. 4:13 BARCLAY) replaces the thought, "I just can't handle this situation. It's too hard!" Replace the lie that there's nothing good ahead for you; you've failed and life is over with the great promise in Jeremiah 29:11–13: "For I know the plans I have for you, says the Lord. They are plans for good and not for evil, to give you a future and a hope. In those days when you pray, I will listen. You will find me when you seek me, if you look for me in earnest" (TLB).

> We can live without fear by building our faith on what God has said in His Word.
>
> Joyce Meyer,
> Help Me, I'm Afraid

Promises like "Greater is He who is in you than he who is in the world" (1 John 4:4 NASB) and "He will give His angels charge concerning you, to guard you in all your ways" (Ps. 91:11 NASB) assure you that the Lord who lives within you is stronger than the enemies about you. And when you feel like nobody cares about you, remember "How precious it is, Lord, to realize that you are thinking about me constantly! I can't even count how many times a day your thoughts turn towards me. And when I waken in the morning, you are still thinking of me" (Ps. 139:17–18 TLB).

Make a Peace Packet. A Peace Packet isn't meant to replace your Bible but to help you apply truth to your life and to remind you that we have a fantastic God who will be faithful to fulfill his promises. Whether your fears relate to your job, your child, your safety, or the future, God's Word applies to *you* and your situation. Here are some suggestions for making and using your own Peace Packet:

- On a 3x5 index card, brightly colored if you prefer, write a verse that has encouraged you or speaks to your situation or fear.
- Repeat the promise in your own words, telling God you are depending on him. For example, "God, you said you would lift the fallen and those bent beneath their loads, that you

are close to all who call on you sincerely (Ps. 145:14–21). Now I trust you to do this in my life."

- Put the cards in a small Ziploc bag to carry with you wherever you go.
- Focus on these truths instead of your fears; read them in the morning and throughout the day, at lunchtime, dinner, or bedtime, whenever you have a few moments.
- Add to the verses in your Peace Packet as you discover more. Ask God each day to show you a new truth.
- Purpose to share a verse with someone each day. Ask God to help you become an encourager and to lead you to someone who needs to hear his Word. When you give the verse away by sharing it with another, it truly becomes your own.

If you would like to order a Peace Packet, contact Heritage Baptist Church (www.heritagefamily.org or 405-720-1449).

Pray God's Word. When we pray the truths and promises of the Bible, we become filled with faith instead of fear and doubt. That's why you'll find Scripture prayers throughout this book. When we pray the verses, whether from a Peace Packet or from a Bible study or from our devotional time, we can trust God to fulfill the promises in his way and timetable. Judson Cornwall says:

> The more we incorporate the Scriptures into our praying, the more likely we are to pray in the will of God, for God always stands behind what He has said . . . When we let the Bible become our prayer, we are praying an inspired vocabulary. It will often release deep inner feelings far better than extemporized prayers that will come from our minds.[4]

Psalm 138:2–3 confirms it: "For your promises are backed by all the honor of your name. When I pray, you answer me, and encourage me by giving me the strength I need" (TLB).

Praying God's promises will comfort your heart, deliver you from fear, and also bear fruit, and that's a promise! God says of his Word, "It will not return to me empty, but will accomplish what I desire and achieve the purpose for which I sent it."

The Lifeline of God's Word

Who shall separate us from the love of Christ? Shall trouble or hardship or persecution or famine or nakedness or danger or sword? . . . No, in all these things we are more than conquerors through him who loved us. For I am convinced that neither death nor life, neither angels nor demons, neither the present nor the future, nor any powers, neither height nor depth, nor anything else in all creation, will be able to separate us from the love of God that is in Christ Jesus our Lord.

Romans 8:35–39

Lord, I thank you that nothing can separate me from your love for me in Christ Jesus. Nothing—trouble, hardship, danger, death, or any powers or force, now or in the future—can remove me from your hand. How I praise you for your forever love that holds me. I pray for a steadfast heart to believe this promise and to confidently stand on it in whatever I face in my life.

Fear not; stand still (firm, confident, undismayed) and see the salvation of the Lord which He will work for you today.

Exodus 14:13 AMP

Lord, strengthen me by your Spirit to stand still and not to fear. Empower me to trust you until I see your salvation worked in my life. I turn from fear to focus on you, for my life to be guided by your Word and not ruled by fear. Thank you that you are with me, and you are mighty and awesome!

five

From Panic to Peace

It is by prayer that we couple the powers of heaven to our helplessness, the powers which can turn water into wine and remove mountains in our own life and in the lives of others.

O. Hallesby

Esther helped her elderly patient settle into a bed in the outpatient oncology center where she served as a nurse. She chatted comfortably while gathering supplies and preparing the medication for the patient's chemotherapy.

All of Esther's patients were favorites, but this woman held a special place in her heart. Even after twenty years of nursing, Esther still prayed each morning for God's wisdom and guidance in treating her patients, and that they would not experience any dangerous side effects. This morning had been no different, and she had confidence of his help.

"Let me check your IV site," she said, making sure the needle was securely in the vein. Then she read each page of the chart to be sure she had all the information she needed. Since the platelet counts were low, Esther called the oncology doctor to verify treatment. He couldn't be reached, but the nurse assured her the doctor had ordered the chemo and two units of blood. Esther turned back to her patient and gently took her hand. Then the medications flowed into the woman's vein.

As the last of the chemo was given, the phone rang. "Whatever you do, *don't* give the patient chemotherapy today. I guess you saw that her counts are too low," said the doctor.

"I already gave her treatment," Esther replied.

"What? How could you be so incompetent?" he screamed. "You'll probably be responsible for this patient's death!"

> A great many people are trying to make peace, but that has already been done. God has not left it for us to do; all we have to do is to enter into it.
>
> *D. L. Moody*

When her husband, Tim, picked Esther up a few hours later to drive to a retreat in a nearby state, she was sick with fear. Her stomach was knotted tightly, and the doctor's tirade still rang in her ears as she thought, *I'll probably go to jail if this patient dies.* This is the nightmare that every nurse hopes and prays will never happen to her—that *her mistake* could kill a patient.

All the way down to the conference center, Esther agonized, "God, how can I pray over my patients and trust you and then have this happen?"

If she dies, I don't know what I'll do. Even if I don't go to jail, I'll lose my nursing license, she thought, her faith shaken to the core. *Can I really trust God at all?* Fear tightened around her until she felt she'd be sick. *She's so precious . . . not just a patient but a friend. I couldn't live with myself if I caused anything to happen to her.* The fear that her patient would die was overwhelming. She couldn't shake it, not even with her husband's encouragement.

By the time they arrived at the conference, Esther was a wreck and deep in the pit of despair. Even though it was warm outside, she felt cold. When she ran into Bill, the retreat speaker and an old friend, the story poured out. "I may be responsible for a patient's death," Esther cried. "I can't think of anything else.

How can I concentrate on the seminars when my patient may be in danger?"

"I think you're at just the right place. Come to the first session I'm doing on fear and worry," Bill encouraged her. After settling their suitcases in the room, Esther reluctantly went to the meeting, doubtful that anything could quell her fears.

In the seminar, Bill explained that he'd always struggled with fear and worry until he discovered the "4 Ps" in Philippians 4:6–8:

Be anxious for nothing, but in everything by prayer and supplication with thanksgiving let your requests be made known to God. And the peace of God, which surpasses all comprehension, will guard your hearts and your minds in Christ Jesus. Finally, brethren, whatever is true, whatever is honorable, whatever is right, whatever is pure, whatever is lovely . . . if there is any excellence and if anything worthy of praise, dwell on these things.

NASB

I know these verses by heart, Esther thought. *I don't see how hearing them again can help me. What am I doing here? I may as well go home and face the consequences.*

"You see," Bill explained, "whenever God commands us to do something—in this case, to be anxious for nothing—to not fear or worry about anything—he always follows with how to do it. So here's what these verses show us to do:

"The first P is to PRAY about what worries you, giving your fear and concerns consciously and specifically to God. Paul is saying in essence, 'Don't have anything to do with anxiety. Stop fearing and start praying!'

"The second P is to PRAISE and thank him for what he will do in the situation. Thank God for the person or situation causing you worry and anxiety because even this very problem is one more reason to trust him.

"The third P is to receive God's PEACE. It's a promise. If you've prayed about the problem and given it to God, then he will move in on your mind and heart with peace through Christ Jesus, because of his work in you."

As Esther took notes, what the speaker was saying began to make sense. Her fear was just as oppressive as when they arrived, but she listened intently as he sketched on the board the remaining *P*:

"The fourth *P* is what to do next. Focus your mind on POSITIVE thoughts about God. Focus on all the wonderful things about his character instead of being preoccupied with negative thoughts, the problematic complications, and how you're going to get out of this mess, or the 'what ifs.' Center your mind firmly on God's goodness."

Praying the 4 Ps

When Esther returned to her room after the seminar, she had a long talk with God. "I've always been able to count on everything in your Word. I'm going to put these verses into practice, regardless of how I feel," she said. She prayed through the 4 Ps, mechanically at first, and gave the whole situation and the patient she was so worried about to God. She prayed for God to pour out his tender mercies and healing power in this woman's life and to protect her and bless her. Thanking him for this awful trial was hard, but when she did, she experienced a few brief minutes of peace.

However, five minutes later, the panic was back again, full force. Over and over again she gave her fears to God, thanked him the best she could for how he was working in her heart and in the situation, and consciously focused on his character, his promises, and his truth. Each time, she received a little bit longer respite of peace. As she continued praying this way, those small blocks of time without fear gradually grew from five minutes to ten and then twenty.

But the next morning when she awoke, Esther's heart was beating wildly and the anxiety was back, stronger than before. *She's going to die. I'm going to prison. Who will care for Tim and our four girls?* She chose to turn to God again and got down on her knees and prayed according to the pattern in Philippians. And this time when the fear returned, it wasn't with as much agony. Throughout the second day and while listening to other messages, she kept giving God her fears, offering her thanks, centering her mind on his faithfulness. Her moments without anxiety grew.

By Sunday, the peace she was experiencing—even before she knew if anything had changed or what news she'd get at the hospital the next day— was so incredible, she couldn't *make* herself worry. Before, when her thoughts wandered to the situation, she was filled with terror. But in those three days of prayer, she had moved from despair and fear to confidence in God—whatever the outcome.

> **If God be our God, He will give us peace in trouble. When there is a storm without, He will make peace within. The world can create trouble in peace, but God can create peace in trouble.**
>
> *Thomas Watson*

Through her experience, God was teaching Esther that she had to trust him, not the circumstances. And amazingly, in the next few weeks, she saw with her own eyes that her patient not only improved, but the cancer went into remission. Although the doctor never admitted that the final dose of chemo had helped turn her condition around, Esther knew God had been at work in her patient's life and physical condition as well as her own.

The pattern of prayer in Philippians 4, casting all her cares, fears, and feelings on God and thanking him in the midst of struggles, cultivated in Esther a deep intimacy with God. Drawing close to him sustained her in the waves of difficulty that hit her life in the next few years: her mother-in-law's massive stroke, which caused her to move in with the family so Esther could become her full-time caretaker; the tragic death of one daughter; the out-of-wedlock pregnancy of another daughter; her husband's cancer, surgery, and recovery process; and their move to another state where God was calling Tim as a pastor.

Instead of panicking in the midst of these situations, Esther prayed, and she found God's incredible peace was always available. Be anxious for nothing—fear nothing—let nothing worry you—covers a lot of ground. It covers fear, guilt, anger, all the things that cause anxiety to well up. Esther realized anxiety and fear are Satan's ballpark. With them, he tries to defeat Christians and stop us from proclaiming God's glory. You can't proclaim God's goodness and glory when you're scared stiff or paralyzed by panic. Yet glorifying God is at the core of our purpose for existing: "You are a chosen race, a royal priesthood, a holy nation, a people for God's own possession, so that you may proclaim the excellencies of Him who has called you out of darkness into His marvelous light" (1 Peter 2:9 NASB).

By handling panic-producing situations with prayer, whether it's a small concern (I'm afraid this hairdresser is ruining my hair!) or a big one (I'm afraid my patient is going to die; I'm afraid my child is going to leave God and the youth group and get into drugs), God—instead of the circumstances—becomes our focus, and peace replaces panic. Wonder replaces worry—wonder at his peace that is more than the human mind can comprehend, wonder at his faithfulness and provision, so that we can "Celebrate God all day, every day . . . revel in him!" (Phil. 4:4 MESSAGE).

A. W. Tozer calls this the "astonished wonder" and awe that is at the heart of true worship. This sense of "spiritual astonishment" happens among men and women when the Holy Spirit is present, working in their lives, just as it happened in Esther's life.

Prayer needs to be our first resource, not a last resort as we face problems, anxiety-producing situations, and just daily life. In our stressful world, prayer is the best thing we can do to relieve stress. Even secular medical research is revealing the anxiety-reducing effects of prayer. Studies at North Carolina's Duke University and elsewhere show that daily prayer is so effective in reducing stress that it cuts women's risk of anxiety by as much as 81 percent. The act of praying triggers biochemical changes in the brain and adds a sense of safety and purpose to our lives.

Catapulted into Prayer

It's amazing that the very things that push our panic buttons can catapult us into earnest prayer, that the very hooks the enemy uses to try to paralyze us with fear can be the springboard to usher us into God's throne room. When people discover that I write and speak on prayer, they ask me, "Have you always been a praying woman? Have you always had a passion for prayer?" They think perhaps I was born on a prayer mountain in Korea to parents who were veteran intercessors and that I loved even as a child to spend hours alone with God praying.

Oh no! Quite the contrary. I was born into a busy family of six kids in Dallas, Texas. Though I have a sister named Martha, I tended to be more "Martha" than she was, the most distracted child busy doing many things. As Mama led us in "Now I lay me down to sleep . . ." every night, I could barely wait for the "Amen" so I could pull out a book I wanted to read or roll my hair up in little pink sponge rollers.

But God apprehended me and brought me into the School of Prayer. He began to develop a "Mary" heart in me alongside my Martha tendencies through my concern for my children, as you'll read in a subsequent chapter. I came to the realization that in this broken world there was much I couldn't control (in fact, control was an illusion), but that my greatest influence for good in my own family and others' lives was *prayer.* I had a huge love for people and hated to see friends, family, or church members suffer physical or any other problems. My heart broke for them. But the Lord showed me the first, best, and most important thing I could do for them was to *pray for them* (and then through praying, he might show me what I could do for them on a practical level).

Prayer became my first resource, not a last resort, as often we treat it. He transformed me from a worrier into a warrior, in prayer, that is. And just like in Esther's life, the pattern of prayer gradually broke my pattern of fear, panic, and worry.

Do I give God my fearful thoughts or problems and leave them perfectly in his hands? No, not always. Many times I take them back and start fretting again, like this little poem "Broken Dreams" expresses:

> As children bring their broken toys
> With tears for us to mend
> I brought my broken dreams to God

Because He was my friend.
But then instead of leaving Him
In peace to work alone,
I hung around and tried to help
With ways that were my own. [ouch, I have done that
    too!]
At last I snatched them back and cried,
"How can You be so slow?"
"My child," He said, "what could I do?
You never did let go."

There Is a Fifth P

That's why we're to PRACTICE, which is the fifth P. Paul says, "Whatever you have learned or received or heard from me, or seen in me—put it into practice." (Don't do this one time and give up if the fear comes back! Keep practicing!) "And the God of peace will be with you."

To practice means giving our concerns to God (and to keep giving them back if we start obsessing over them again); to practice means thanking him in the midst of difficulties because it's another chance for him to show himself mighty and faithful in our lives; to practice means receiving his peace and dwelling on the positive instead of the negative. God is calling us to give them all to him—our shattered dreams, deepest burdens, fears, and pain. He can handle them, transforming your fear into faith, your panic into peace. It's kind of like just pouring out water from a pitcher—we pour out these burdens and problems and God pours in his peace, joy, and love. So keep pouring! Keep practicing! Keep praying!

In the simple act of giving your fears and problems to the Lord, you will experience his presence, which is far more wonderful than we can imagine; you will have a changed perspective; you will come into more intimacy with God as you draw near to him in your difficulty—for he promises to draw near to you (James 4:8).

Faith Builders

We each have different "panic buttons" and certain experiences that shake our lives. Sometimes it's a single calamitous event, like the death of a spouse, a job loss, or the threat of such a loss. Other times misfortune comes as it did in Job's life—an earthquake of tragedy plus waves of difficulty and pain. For Esther the possibility of a patient dying because of her actions triggered overwhelming anxiety. But no matter what your particular panic button is, the 5 Ps will work, but not because they are a magic formula. They work because when we put God's Word into practice and lay the tracks down in prayer for his power to come, we emerge from darkness and fear into his marvelous light and hope. Here's how to start:

The moment fear hits, go right to God. Pull away wherever you are and get into God's presence. That means at work, driving down the freeway (keep your eyes open), even in the midst of a conversation—take the worry to him instead of engaging it in your mind and thinking of all the terrible things that could happen. When something bad happens that causes fear, we have a tendency to blame God for allowing us to go through the difficulty. When we blame God and turn away from him, Satan has a heyday with our thoughts. Our mind becomes his playground. That's why Paul tells us to "take captive every thought to make it obedient to Christ" (2 Cor. 10:5). And regardless of what the situation is, begin to thank God about how he has blessed you recently and

- how he is drawing you to him through this fear or problem
- what he is going to do in the situation
- how you are going to grow
- how God is going to reveal himself in your need or concern

As you choose to turn to God, thank him, and begin to praise him, it delights his heart. All of life tries to pull you down into circumstances, but when you focus on the Lord, he blesses you with the ability to cope victoriously with a problem. At the same time, Satan and his doubts and discouragement will begin to flee from you.

"Thanksgiving gives effect to prayer," said Robert Jamieson, "and frees us from anxious carefulness by making all God's dealings a matter for praise, not merely for resignation, much less murmuring. Peace is the companion of thanksgiving."[1]

> Through faith you have become a child of God, you have been saved, and through faith you also achieve victory over worry, fear, and other sins. Cast your burdens on the Lord. You do that when you pray.
>
> *Corrie ten Boom*

Persist and don't give up. What if you've prayed through the 5 Ps and given your worry to God and it comes back a few minutes later? Don't give up. That's why the fifth *P* is "practice." Remember that the bigger or heavier the fear or problem, the more times you may need to give it to God until you have really let go of it. If the fear recurs, don't say, "Well, this isn't working." Instead, stop and give your worry to God again. Each time you release it, you'll get a little more victory. Each time, peace will increase until your mind is *at rest* concerning the matter. *Rest* means mental and spiritual tranquility, freedom from worry. And that's often when the creative solution or insight of what you can do about your problem, if anything, will come to mind—when you are mentally and emotionally resting.

Receive his peace. Philippians 4:7 says, "The peace of God, which surpasses all comprehension, will guard your hearts and your minds in Christ Jesus" (NASB). Claiming God's peace is a matter of yielding to him and receiving what he freely offers. Peace isn't what you conjure up to make yourself feel better about the situation. It's not affirming self-talk but claiming the peace of Almighty God—a peace we can't fathom or measure— that will transform your very thoughts. Christ's whole nature is peace. He is the Prince of Peace.

The Message's translation of that verse says, "Before you know it, a sense of God's wholeness, everything coming together for good, will come and settle you down. It's wonderful what happens when *Christ displaces worry at the center of your life*" (italics mine). And isn't it amazing that the problem doesn't have to go away for us to experience this peace? Yes, we want it to be resolved (in fact, I have found that we often just get a new set of problems when one is solved). But we aren't promised a problem-free life. We're promised that God will give us the power and peace to live abundantly even in the midst of adversity.

Pray with others. There's nothing better than to join hearts and hands in prayer with other believers about the things we are most concerned about. God didn't mean for us to be Lone Ranger Christians, slugging it out against the enemy in our solitary way. When the battle is fierce or long, we naturally get discouraged and need other sisters and brothers in Christ to pray with us—and they will need us to lift them up for their concerns too. Even the great leader Moses needed Aaron and Hur to support him and hold his arms up in prayer as he interceded for the Israelites when they were battling against the Amalekites (see Exod. 17). And you and I need prayer partners too: a group of women to pray with, or sometimes a whole network of prayer, like churchwide intercession in a time of crisis. God is calling all of us to pray about our families' lives and what's going on in our nation and in the world. Join the army of intercessors and bring others with you!

Let prayer become a way of life. The "practice these things" part of the Philippians passage can remind us to pray using the 5 Ps in the small anxieties and the larger fears every day. Prayer opens the door to the One who can save us from our fears and redeem our situation. As you practice prayer, giving your concerns and burdens to God will become as natural as breathing. Just as soldiers in warfare practice their maneuvers and strategies so they are ready to use them in real combat, practice these 5 Ps so you'll be ready when your personal battle comes:

Pray
Praise
Peace
Positive thoughts
Practice, practice, practice

To start a new pattern, write the 5 P words on a card to carry with you or to post on the refrigerator along with Philippians 4:6–9. This will remind you every day to release your fears to God in prayer. As you make the 5 Ps a part of your lifestyle, you'll find the 5 Ds, Dread, Doubt, Depression, Despondency, and Disease, will disappear. It's in practice that the truth of Philippians 4 will move from your head to your heart, that the joy of the Lord will be the strength you need not just to survive but to worship God with an astonished sense of wonder and enjoy him right in the midst of whatever you're going through.

The Lifeline of God's Word

Casting the whole of your care [all your anxieties, all your worries, all your concerns, once and for all] on Him; for He cares for you affectionately and cares about you watchfully.

1 Peter 5:7 AMP

Lord, thank you that you invite me to roll upon you, casting just like a fisherman casts his line into the lake, all my worries and fears, all the things that concern me because you love me affectionately and care for me. I give you my deepest cares now. . . .

Peace I leave with you; My [own] peace I now give and bequeath to you. Not as the world gives do I give to you. Do not let your hearts be troubled, neither let them be afraid. [Stop allowing yourselves to be agitated and disturbed; and do not permit yourselves to be fearful and intimidated and cowardly and unsettled.]

John 14:27 AMP

Lord, I admit my heart has been troubled and afraid. Help me to choose to turn to you instead of staying agitated and fretting about my problem. You have given your peace and I receive it and thank you for it! What a wonderful gift! I don't have to live fearful and unsettled, but I can be free and experience your peace and joy.

SiX

Acceptance: The Door to Peace

In returning [to Me] and resting [in Me] you shall be saved;
in quietness and in [trusting] confidence shall be your strength.

Isaiah 30:15 AMP

Marilyn was exhausted the morning she and her husband, Dave, came home from the center where he had received treatment for alcoholism for thirty days. Every day for a month she'd been handling not only their three children but fielding calls from bill collectors, operating a car pool, working at a part-time job, and trying to run the household by herself. Dave emerged in better shape than he'd been in months. Marilyn, however, was a wreck.

In her room that morning she cried and even yelled at God, "I've prayed since 1989 about our finances, and look what's happened!" Her tirade continued as she looked over her journal entries and the Scriptures she had prayed, claimed, and clung to in the past year. She looked at the stack of bills she couldn't pay and sobbed in discouragement. "I just don't believe you anymore!" she told God.

Marilyn was angry at God for all the prayers she felt went unanswered, angry at friends for not confronting Dave with his alcoholism sooner, before it wrecked his career and their bank account, mad at Dave for getting them in trouble and for his addiction, and angry at herself for putting up with the awful situation and allowing it to disrupt their kids and family.

> Our Lord, our God, deliver us from the fear of what might happen. And give us the grace to enjoy what now is and to keep striving after what ought to be.
>
> *Peter Marshall*

But most of all, she was terrified about what they were going to do now that her mate was sober but out of a job. How would they pay the huge pile of bills? As Dave passed their bedroom and saw Marilyn on the floor, he asked, "What's the matter with you?"

"What's wrong with *me*? Everything! But right now I don't understand these finances and why we can't ever pay our bills. I've trusted God and he's let me down," Marilyn answered, tears flowing down her cheeks.

"Remember, acceptance is the answer to all your problems," Dave said, glibly reiterating a principle he'd learned at the center as he walked out to the garage to work on the car.

You mean I'm supposed to accept that we don't have any money, that you're an alcoholic, that our life has crashed? she thought, continuing to sob. Then as she sat there in the quiet and began to think about it, she realized her focus was always so fixed on when Dave was going to change and when their financial problems were going to be solved that she had never accepted anything. She had tried to control things and fix him, even taking over paying the bills so it would be done on time. She had memorized many verses of Scripture, expecting that someday their financial situation was going to be perfect, that they would be able to buy a house, and that God was going to fix everything she couldn't. But when it didn't happen that way, she was crushed by disappointment and paralyzed by fear about what they were going to do.

She kept praying for those things she wanted and kept looking to the future when her prayers would be answered with what she thought was the ideal solution. But it never happened! Marilyn's life was like what C. S. Lewis described in the movie *Shadowlands:* "We live in the shadowlands. The sun is always shining somewhere else, around the bend in the road, over the brow of a hill." And her eyes were fixed right over that hill!

So that day Marilyn got out her journal and began to write, "Acceptance is the answer to all my problems today." She wrote down all the problems she faced and all the fears and anxieties she had about them. *Lord, I've prayed, tithed, worked, and nothing has opened up to us. I know that if you wanted to, you could change things in a moment or a day. But you haven't. So I accept the way things are today, the things I can't change. I want you to show me what you're doing. I want to see you and trust you in the midst of our problems today, in the here and now.*

For the first time in a long time, peace slowly began to replace the anxiety and worry she was feeling. In the process of writing, she remembered what God had done even in the last few months. The "wilderness blessings" they had received were many. They were living in a rented house, but it was a large, lovely one, and the owners had allowed them to live there rent free for the time Dave was in the treatment center and until they recovered financially. She recalled the friends who had supported and helped them; the ones who brought meals, the friend who gave her clothes when she had no money to buy any for herself. She also began to see that God was doing something in her and her husband, teaching them a deeper level of responsibility and changing them both.

Until now she had been just like the Israelites complaining about the manna God had provided in the wilderness. While she was looking down the road from the Shadowlands, she had missed the things God was doing today. Her anxiety and anger dissipated as acceptance and gratefulness grew.

As Hannah Hurnard said, the only way to live victoriously in the midst of life's difficulties is

> by learning to accept, day by day, the actual conditions and tests permitted by God, by a continually repeated laying down of our own will and acceptance of His as it is presented to us in the form of the people with whom we have to live and work, and in the things which happen to us. Every acceptance of His will becomes an altar of sacrifice, and every such surrender and abandonment of ourselves to His will is a means of furthering us on the way to the High Places to which He desires to bring every child of His while they are still living on earth.[1]

When Emotions Overwhelm

From that point, whenever Marilyn began getting anxious or emotional about any situation, she repeated the process that brought her to acceptance. Her circumstances didn't usually change overnight, but she learned to walk in a daily peace and rest in God right in the middle of her problems. Now whatever she faces, she gets her journal out and starts a new page, writing at the top: "Acceptance is the answer to all my problems today."

She then lists the needs and problems that are causing her the most fear or frustration. Then she thinks of what God would have her to do, what action she should take, and writes it down. One day she realized she needed to stop charging on her credit cards; on another day, she knew she needed to call a financial counselor and ask for help. Once when she asked God what he wanted her to do, his answer was very practical: Make a budget and live by it. These were things she *could* change that might make a difference.

Then Marilyn journals about the things she can't change that day. From doing this she has learned that if a nagging irritation with a person or a situation persists, it's probably a good indication that she isn't accepting things. For example, when she was constantly irritated that her husband wasn't a sharp dresser and put together things she thought looked bad, she realized she wasn't accepting him. Or once when a house they were living in was a continual burr under her saddle, then she knew she wasn't accepting it as God's present provision.

As she lists the issues, it helps her think through them: Can I change that in any way? Have I prayed about it? Could God change it if he wanted to? Have I asked him to show me my part to do? Is he asking me to do something? Is God listening? Am I listening?

Then she writes down what God's Word has to say about those matters, noting the verses that come to mind. For example, to address her fear about whether God is listening, she wrote: "God has surely listened and heard my voice in prayer. Praise be to God, who has not rejected my prayer or withheld his love from me" (Ps. 66:19–20). To address the issue of the house she didn't like and was afraid she was going to be stuck in forever: "I have learned to be content in whatever circumstances I am," Paul said, ". . . to get along with humble means, and I also know how to live in prosperity . . . both of having abundance and suffering need" (Phil. 4:11–12 NASB) and "Godliness actually is a means of great gain when accompanied by contentment" (1 Tim. 6:6 NASB).

She used the Psalms to praise God, not to get him to do what she wanted but to express her love and thankfulness. "True praise is not an attempt to manipulate God into producing the precise results we hope for," says Ruth Myers. "Instead it helps us accept our situation as it is, whether or not he changes it. And if we continue praising God, it helps us reach the place where we can

> Two women looked through prison bars
> One saw mud, the other saw stars . . .
>
> Each of us has a choice about how we look at life: We can focus on the mud or lift our eyes and see the stars. Every woman has circumstances that appear to be prison bars. God wants you and me to learn to be content *in* our circumstances, not when they improve.
>
> *Linda Dillow,* Calm My Anxious Heart

say, 'Father, I don't want You to remove this problem until You've done all You want to do through it, in me and others.'" James 1:4 underscores this thought, "Don't try to get out of anything prematurely. Let it do its work so you become mature and well-developed, not deficient in any way" (MESSAGE).

What Acceptance Is and Isn't

Sometimes we equate "acceptance" with an attitude of "anything goes": *I'll accept any behavior my husband or children dish out.* Instead, acceptance is embracing and dealing with the problem behavior while loving the person. For example, if you discover your son has a drug problem, acceptance is admitting and acknowledging that he has a drug problem. Nonacceptance of that fact is denial. If you are accepting the problem, you are

- there to get him help, which may involve loving confrontation and arranging for treatment
- accepting him as a person, but not excusing his inappropriate behavior
- setting boundaries at home
- listening to the needs of his heart and praying for him

All the while, you are loving him unconditionally in his difficulty (because people need love the most when they are the most unlovable) and doing whatever common sense, God's wisdom, and reliable counsel advise you to do. None of the above includes being a doormat for your son or enabling his unacceptable behavior and drug abuse to continue.

Acceptance doesn't mean you quit praying and resign yourself to a negative future; it doesn't mean becoming irresponsible or giving up. While it isn't any of these things, it is realizing that you can trust God—trust him to bring an answer, though perhaps not the answer you'd expected, *and* to weave things into a pattern for good even out of the most trying situation or problem. If there is nothing you can do to change today's situation, acceptance is trusting God to get you through anything. Acceptance is facing the storms of life with God's peace. It will bring you into the reality of the *now* (instead of the far off or fantasy) and allow you to see more of what God is doing and what he is calling you to today. At the same time, walking in this kind of acceptance and trust in God will drain away fear and anxiety.

From Control to Rest

I have found that the more control we try to exert, the more fear builds, and the more fear builds, the more we try to control instead of giving ourselves to surrender, rest, and acceptance. How do we get out of this control/fear trap? Francois Fénelon, in his wonderful volume of letters titled *Let Go,* written in the seventeenth century and yet just as alive and applicable today as it was then, captures the spirit of acceptance: "If you recognize the hand of God and make no opposition to His will, you will have peace in the midst of affliction. Happy indeed are they who can bear their sufferings with this simple peace and perfect submission to the will of God."[2]

How can you and I experience this kind of quietness and confidence instead of fear in the midst of crisis? How can we face whatever comes with acceptance rather than resignation? A look at the story of Shadrach, Meschach, and Abednego in Daniel 3 gives us a model. The three young Israelite men were being thrown into the fiery furnace because they refused to bow to the Babylonian idols. They faced a terrible crisis as severe as any we might ever encounter in life. And if God didn't come and deliver them, they would surely die. Here's how they were able to walk through the trial without fear: In addition to all their prayers and worship of the living God, they had made a commitment:

(They) replied to the king, "O Nebuchadnezzar, we do not need to defend ourselves before you in this matter. If we are thrown into the blazing furnace, the God we serve is able to save us from it, and he will rescue us from your hand. . . .

But even if he does not, we want you to know, O king, that we will not serve your gods or worship the image of gold you have set up."

Daniel 3:16–18

David Wilkerson, pastor of the Times Square Church in New York City, concludes that we are always to pray in faith, believing that God will answer, yet trust him completely with our situation, saying in our hearts, "But if not, Lord, I'm still going to trust You!"[3]

That's acceptance at its deepest level: knowing Christ Jesus will come into our crisis and walk through it with us. When we yield ourselves to him and his will and trust that whatever happens, he is faithful and will never leave us or forsake us. The peace and freedom from fear that comes with this kind of confidence in God is sufficient for any of our earthly trials.

Faith Builders

Acceptance says, "True, this is my situation at the moment. I'll look unblinkingly at the reality of it. But I'll also open my hands to accept whatever a loving Father sends. Thus acceptance never slams the door on hope."[4] Here are some steps to take toward accepting your situation:

> Faith is . . .
> **Letting go of my demands that another change and looking to God for the change He sees I need.**
>
> *Pamela Reeve, Faith Is . . .*

Write in your journal the things and people in your life, including their behaviors, that you have the hardest time accepting. Take a good, honest look at not only what you have difficulty accepting but also what fears are connected to each. Then ask God, "What are you asking me to do regarding each problem? What do you want me to take action on?" Ask the Lord to show you what's *your part*, what's *his part*, and what's *your spouse's part* (or the other person's part), so you don't try to do everyone else's part, thus blocking their growth. Then write what God's Word has to say about each issue. Go to the concordance in your Bible for help in discovering wisdom to apply to these situations. Store up God's truth in your heart and then talk to him about it by turning these verses into prayers as the Holy Spirit leads you.

Shift from questioning or demanding of God, "When are you going to take this problem away?" to asking him, "What is it you are shaping in my life through this trial or difficulty? What can I learn from this experience?" Ask God to show you what he wants to teach *you.* (Oh, how the Lord is often just waiting for us to ask this so he can show us what we need to know or understand!) A humble, teachable attitude also diffuses the little nagging fears and minimizes the frustrations we feel when the wilderness season continues long after when we feel it should be over.

It reminds me of what Andrew Murray suggested we say in time of trouble:

First, the Lord brought me here. It is by His will I am in this strait place; in that will I rest.

Next, He will keep me in His love and give me grace in this trial to behave as His child.

Then, He will make the trial a blessing, teaching me the lessons He means me to learn and working in me the grace He intends for me.

Last, in His good time He can bring me out again, how and when He knows.[5]

Murray encourages us to remind ourselves, *I am here: by God's appointment, in God's keeping, under his training, for his time.* I have to admit that in the midst of some of my own personal crises, this seemed a hard message to hear. But the more I have pondered Murray's advice, the more I have realized that my situation doesn't take God by surprise and that there *will be a time he brings me through it,* and that he will use it to shape and mold me to be more like Christ, fitting me not only for his purposes but also preparing me for what he has ahead. Knowing these things encourages me and helps me to embrace God's will instead of resisting and resenting it.

Cultivate a sense of humor, a lightheartedness about yourself and your problems. Sometimes this is hardest for us serious Christians who are burdened and anxious about a circumstance. Try—ask the Holy Spirit's help—to laugh at yourself once in a while. When we take ourselves and our issues too seriously, we become difficult to live with and lose perspective. A lively sense of humor helps us accept ourselves and become more accepting of others. It is *good news* that God loves and accepts us in spite of our messes and failures. Pray for that kind of "love that covers" for yourself and the people close to you.

Develop a sense of gratitude and wonder about life. Don't forget to write in your journal, as Marilyn did, things God has done that you can thank him for or gifts he has given in your wilderness season or trial. Each day is a gift of God that we haven't earned or deserved, so there is always something to thank him for, always something to celebrate even if things are pretty difficult: the beauty of a glowing purple-and-red sunset when you've been sitting in a stuffy, colorless hospital all day holding the hand of a critically ill friend; finding an unexpected "I love you, Mom" note from your teen who has been giving you trouble, a juicy piece of watermelon on a hot day. Just like the wonder you felt long ago about Christmas, take delight in God's blessings, large and small, every day no matter what the difficulties are.

The Lifeline of God's Word

And be satisfied with your present [circumstances and with what you have]; for He [God] Himself has said, I will not in any way fail you nor give you up nor leave you without support. [I will] not, [I will] not, [I will] not in any degree leave you helpless nor forsake nor let [you] down (relax my hold on you). [Assuredly not!] So we take comfort and are encouraged and confidently and boldly say The Lord is my Helper; I will not be seized with alarm [I will not fear or dread or be terrified]. What can man do to me?

Hebrews 13:5–6 AMP, italics mine

Lord, grant me your grace to be satisfied with what I have and be accepting of my present circumstances, knowing that you will not fail me or forsake me ever, that you will always support me and that you are for me. Nothing can happen to me apart from your loving hand. I take comfort and am encouraged, and I want to say with confidence, you are my helper! I will not fear or be terrified!

Do you want more and more of God's kindness and peace? Then learn to know him better and better. For as you know him better and better, he will give you, through his great power, everything you need for living a truly good life: he even shares his own glory and his own goodness with us! And by that same mighty power he has given us all the other rich and wonderful blessings he promised.

2 Peter 1:2–4 TLB

Lord, I want to know you more and know more of your kindness and peace, but most of all, I want to know YOU! Open my eyes to see you in my world and situation. Thank you for giving me everything I need for living a truly good life, and thank you for sharing your own glory and goodness with me. Thank you that by your power you have given me all the other rich and wonderful blessings you have promised. How can I not trust you, such a great God that you are!

seven

Overcoming Fears about Our Children

Prayer, even prayer for what God desires, releases power by the operation of a deep spiritual law; and to offer up what one loves may release still more.

Sheldon Vanaken

Dread tied my stomach in knots before I ever opened my eyes that September Sunday morning. Even in deep sleep I listened for the sound that sparked fear in me. The rattling sound was all the scarier because it emanated from the chest of my six-year-old son, Justin.

His skin was pale and drawn, his chest heaved as he gasped for a breath. I looked into his blue eyes and saw a reflection of my own fears.

Scrambling out of bed, I ran for his inhaler. Asthma had become the embodiment of every fear I owned. I'd tried so hard to protect my children, giving them nutritious meals and vitamins, hovering over them like a quail with her covey. My husband, Holmes, thought I was being overprotective, and I knew

I was. But how could I explain the horrible dread that welled up in me, especially when our firstborn was sick?

When asthma hit Justin at age four, it hadn't been a simple case of wheezing. His first attack had been full-blown *status asthmaticus*. It took days in a hospital to bring his breathing back to normal.

That's what I hated most about asthma—I was powerless to control it. An attack could hit at any moment, changing our plans. This chronic illness had stolen my joy and overtaken our life. It had even curtailed our travel to the grandparents' ranch in Texas because we'd wind up in an emergency room due to the climate change.

> **Through prayer we can open a window to God's love.**
>
> *Unknown*

Just as we always did, we consulted with the doctor on the phone that day, gave Justin all his medicine, and made sure he used his inhaler and rested. But this time nothing worked. Even with careful nursing, as the day grew longer his wheezing worsened.

By 10 P.M. we dropped our two younger children at a neighbor's and sped to the hospital emergency room in the rain. Several injections of adrenaline and IV medications didn't snap Justin out of the attack, so the ER doctor called our pediatrician. When I saw our own doctor stride down the long, gray hall, I breathed a sigh of relief. *I just know he can get Justin's asthma attack under control. He always has before.*

"Raise the level of aminophyllin and cortisone. Give him another adrenalin injection," he ordered the ER nurses. "An asthma attack is like a ball rolling down a hill," Dr. Spencer told us. "We've got to stop it with the biggest guns available before it gets any closer to the bottom. Don't worry—you'll probably be home in a few hours." He turned on his heels and disappeared down the hall.

But at 2 A.M. the nurse called Holmes and me out of the ER cubicle. "Your son is not responding as well as he should be. You'll have to admit him to the hospital. If you'll just go down the hall to 'Admitting' and sign the papers, we'll get him upstairs to a room."

Dashed Hopes

My spirits fell like the rain pelting the window beside me. Swallowing a huge lump in my throat, I thought about the yellow Snoopy lunch box Justin had picked out, the new jeans and red plaid shirt already laid out on his bunk bed for the first big day. "Holmes, there's no way he'll be well enough to start school!"

"I think we have a lot more to worry about than school," he bristled. After we got our son all settled in his fifth-floor room, Holmes sent me home to stay with Alison and Chris while he kept vigil next to Justin's bedside. I just *knew* he'd be better in the morning.

But when I walked in at 8 A.M., Justin was white-faced, an oxygen tube in his nose. The muscles in his neck and chest strained as he fought for air. Every breath sounded like a rib-rattling staccato. In spite of other treatments, his condition worsened throughout the day. On his afternoon rounds, Dr. Spencer examined him again, shook his head, and took us out in the hall.

"Something inside his body has got to rally. I've done everything I know to do," he told us.

Stunned, I couldn't believe what I heard. My heart raced. The rising anxiety cracked the thin veneer of calm I had tried so hard to maintain.

"Why don't you go home for a while?" Holmes said.

"But I can't leave now."

"You've got to nurse Alison and reassure Chris. They haven't seen you for hours. Besides, you aren't much help unless you pull yourself together. You're only making him nervous," he said.

I hated to leave, but I knew he was right. In a dazed fog, I rode the elevator down and walked out the front door of the hospital. A loud clap of thunder startled me. A slap of cold rain stung my face. I searched up and down the rows of parked cars but couldn't find our station wagon anywhere. Finally, soaked and shivering, I was driven back into the hospital by the rain to wait for the storm to let up. Huddling next to the door, I noticed the sign: "Chapel."

Reluctantly, I slipped into the empty chapel and was drawn to the large white Bible at the front, open to Psalm 42:

> Why are you downcast, O my soul?
> Why so disturbed within me?
> Put your hope in God,
>   for I will yet praise him,
>   my Savior and my God.
>
> Psalm 42:5–6

Finally, in the quiet, I prayed, "Lord, I've put my hope in the doctor, the medicine, Holmes, and myself to save Justin. That's why I'm in so much despair and fear. I've trusted you in some areas of my life, but I've clung to my kids, trying to keep them safe. I even dedicated them in a church service, but I never really entrusted them totally to your care. I'm like the disciples who, in the midst of a fierce storm, cried out to Jesus, 'Master, Master, we are perishing!'"

And a quiet inner voice said to me, as he had to the disciples, "Cheri, where is your faith? Peace . . . be still."

Lightning caused the chapel lights to flicker off and on, and thunder boomed outside, turning my thoughts again to God:

The Creator of the whole universe—in complete command of the thunderstorm outside, yet I couldn't trust him with my son's life. In not releasing him to God's care, I'm thwarting the very power that could help him.

"Hope in ME," I felt him say. "Trust his life to me totally."

I bowed my head and this time said, "Father, forgive me for not trusting him to your care sooner. I forgot that he was your child first and that you made him. I give him to you whatever happens."

As I walked outside, something warm began to melt away that icy fear that had gripped me. The torrent of rain had turned to a drizzle. After searching several rows in the parking lot, I found our car.

I drove up the hill to get on the expressway. When I slowed at the yield sign, I looked up and was struck by a tiny sliver of terrifically bright sunshine that broke through the angry, black clouds.

At that moment, a huge weight lifted inside me, and a feeling of peace unlike I'd ever experienced swept through me. Justin was safe and cared for. In some inexplicable way I knew it, and I knew I could trust God with our precious firstborn son.

I spent a happy, unhurried hour with Chris and Alison in our favorite yellow rocking chair at home, munching cheese and crackers and reading *Richard Scarry* books to them.

> We survive the packages of pain God allows in our lives by remembering who God is and what He has done in the past.
>
> *Linda Dillow,* Calm My Anxious Heart

An hour and a half later I returned to the hospital and walked into our son's room. He was sitting up in bed, coloring a picture and chatting with his grandparents who had just arrived from East Texas. A smile lit up his rosy face as he asked, "Mom, when can I go home and see Chris and Alison and puppy?"

Although Justin still battled asthma in the years to come, his treatment never required hospitalization again. When I packed his Snoopy lunch box on his first day of school, I sent him off with a deep sense of peace. I wouldn't be there to protect him.

But I knew the One who would.

And it wasn't only healing in our son that took place that day but also healing in me because my focus changed from the afflicting problem to God. As I saw him anew as the all-powerful, almighty Lord for whom nothing is too difficult, as I experienced his love in the midst of our crisis, the tight grip fear had over me was broken. Just as God reached down inside Justin's body to restore his breathing and oxygen level, he reached deep inside me into my heart and emotions to restore trust. Never again did I respond in panic when Justin had another asthma attack. My response was different because over and over God's perfect love cast out fear. As the years passed, our son still had asthma but grew stronger each year. He was a varsity tennis player for his high school and in his twenties became a long-distance runner for whom marathons were a breeze—even completing rugged fifty-mile trail runs. God has surprises around the bend as we trust him!

Losing Control

Oh, how we wish we could control things so everything goes smoothly for us and our kids, so they wouldn't have problems and neither would we, if we could just manage it all. For years, Dana had prided herself on being organized, self-sufficient, and "in control" of many aspects of her life. Although she knew God, she wasn't placing her trust fully in him but in her ability to keep everything together. And then she began to experience a series of adversities.

Within five years, their home was threatened by the five-hun-dred-year Red River flood, her daughter fell twelve feet from the balcony of their home, Dana experienced acute health problems related to a bad gallbladder, and her husband's business was threatened by the events of 9-11 and the weakening economy. During this time they also had some uninvited visitors to their home, a home she had kept immaculately clean. Lice! Twice! It's amazing how quickly something so small can disarm a woman who believes that she is in control of her life.

Any peace that may have come from her organizational skills and self-sufficiency soon melted away as Dana realized she was in control of absolutely nothing. She came to the end of herself, however, when their three-year-old son, Soren, began experi-encing unusual spells of abdominal pain followed by lethargy and unconsciousness.

At the same time that she was grieving her only son's loss of health, she was beginning to experientially understand that the Lord cared about her, that he alone knew what her needs were, and that he would provide the exact measure of what she needed to get through each day, minute by minute. One of those provi-sions came in the form of a gift from a friend who gave her the original version of this book. As she read about my experience of placing my son in God's strong hands and the truth of Philip-pians 4:6–9, she began to see that in all things, she could:

Pray about what concerned her and consciously give it to God
Praise him for what he will do in the situation
Receive God's peace
Focus her mind on thoughts about God

As they received the news that their little son had a rare vascular malformation of the liver that was virtually undocumented in the history of medical literature, Dana was driven to her knees in agony and despair. At this point she realized she had to make a decision. Was she willing to place her trust in the Lord? Would she confidently entrust the Lord with Soren?

As she prayed about her concerns for Soren, praised the Lord for his power at work in his life, received God's peace, and focused her mind on the greatness and sovereignty of God, she was filled with an overwhelming sense of peace, confidence, and hope—and was able to confidently release her son into the Lord's hands. Little did she know that this would be the beginning of a journey that is now more than five years in the making. Has God delivered them out of the adversity? No—in fact, just a few weeks ago Dana received a call at 9:30 in the morning from Soren's school saying he had become listless during his gym class.

Dana dropped what she was doing and drove twenty minutes to the school. When she arrived, Soren was stable. As he was leaving the office to return to class, he had another spell of lethargy. By this time, it was 11:00, and Dana needed to take her husband to the airport at noon because he was leaving the country for a conference.

It seemed best for Soren to spend the afternoon at home. As Dana was driving, her mind was flooded with questions. *Should I take him to the emergency room? How serious is this? Should Thor leave for this conference today?* Then she remembered she was scheduled to leave town in less than forty-eight hours to assist in a weekend ministry event in Tampa, Florida. How could she possibly get on a plane and leave Soren in the hands of friends while both she and her husband would be out of town?

As she confided her fears about leaving to her prayer partner, her friend told her, "You really need to hear from the Lord on this. I will pray specifically that you will hear from him as to whether or not you should go to Tampa." As Dana came to the Lord in prayer and continued reading the Word, she was assured he would reveal his will.

The next morning as she meditated on Psalm 102 from her daily readings, the last verse of the chapter touched her deeply. "The children of your people will live in security. Their children's children will thrive in your presence" (v. 28 NLT). Although this verse brought comfort, she was still not sure that she had definitively heard from God as to whether or not she should go to Tampa.

Later that morning as she attended Bible study, the leader spoke from the fourth chapter of John. Dana had completed her study preparation earlier in the week, prior to Soren's spells, and the troubles had chased it out of her memory. So she wasn't prepared for the amazing new way the Lord would speak to her during the lecture. As the leader read John 4:50, Dana was awestruck. In this verse Jesus says, "You may go. Your son will live."

It was immediately apparent to Dana, and to the friend sitting next to her who had also been praying for her, that the Lord had clearly spoken and she was to go to Tampa. And go she did. Soren had a wonderful weekend with their friends and had no health problems while she was gone.

Five years into this journey with Soren's health problems, Dana is still learning to trust in the Lord with all her heart. Time and time again she is learning that it is *only* as she practices praising, focusing on the Lord through prayer and the study of his Word, and receiving his peace that she has received strength for the day and hope for the future.

From Fear to Faith

As mothers, we have a desire to protect and care for our children that seems to come with the job description. But sometimes that caring can turn to clinging. A crisis occurs. Your child is hospitalized. The television news flashes a picture of a child kidnapped in your state. You become preoccupied with what might happen. You check every hour during the night to see if your baby is still breathing. You don't trust anyone to baby-sit. Or as a mom of teenagers, you are constantly anxious about your daughter or son getting in with the wild crowd. When these kinds of fears plague you, here are some ways to move from fear to faith:

Release your children into God's loving hands. Praying the prayer of relinquishment as Dana and I did, essentially entrusting your kids to God, is rarely easy. In fact, I think "letting go" is perhaps the hardest work of motherhood, and it may happen in a watershed moment or step-by-step. However it occurs, releasing them to God does open a door for the Lord's power and presence to come into our children's lives and situations, and in the process we begin to be freed from our fears.

> **Lord, help me to remember that nothing is going to happen today that You and I can't handle.**
>
> *Unknown*

And whether you never have to go through a medical crisis with your child or not, there is a time for all of us when God asks us to do what Hannah and Abraham did with their children: give him what we love the most.

As Karen Mains says,

> It's important for parents to walk to this spiritual altar, to offer their children back to the Lord. For many of us, this begins when they are infants. We give them to God in a dedicatory service or through a christening ceremony. We give them up to the Lord, sometimes on that first day of school watching them walk away from home, looking so small, so vulnerable before the enormous destructive forces that range the world. We suddenly realize we are not all-powerful but are dependent upon supernatural intervention to protect our children from oncoming cars, from cruelty on the playground, from harsh teachers. At each point of our children's growth, they leave us by degrees, and we must learn to give them again into God's hands.[1]

One way to move toward the goal of releasing your fears *and* your kids to God is to reflect on how faithful he has been in your lives in the past and make a list of all his past goodness. Deena, a mother of three, hadn't ever been fearful until she had children. All that changed when her infant Caitlin's lungs burst due to pulmonary hypertension and she had to be airlifted in critical condition to a Houston hospital. At that point, Deena realized how little control she had, and she was able to entrust her baby's medical problems to God's care. But when she got Caitlin home after many weeks in the hospital, this young mother found herself protective and clingy.

When fear and worry started to grip her again, Deena made a habit of jotting down on paper all God's past goodness in their lives. "Doing this reminds me who my children are, who God is, and what he's done," she says.

"I remind myself they are God's children, and I'm more a caretaker for them than an owner—there's a big difference! He's *their* heavenly Father, the One who created them and promises he'll work everything in their lives for a pattern of good. And then I think of the many answered prayers, how Caitlin recovered, of the blessings that came out of difficult times . . ."

As Deena continues listing God's goodness in this way, it's as if he loosens her grip, finger by finger, on the situation *and* the fear so she can trust him in the present. As she says, "Sometimes I have as tight a grip on fear as it does on me!" Then she's freer to open her hands and heart, lay her children and their problems before God, and experience his comforting presence.

Meditate on Scripture to help keep your focus on the truth instead of the things that are worrying you. Each week pick one verse that specifically applies to your children or your concerns about them and add it to your Peace Packet. (See the verses at the end of this chapter to help you get started.) God's promises remind you how much he cares for you and your children. They help you remember that the One who created your children loves them more than you ever could and that they are secure in his loving, strong hands. His Word gives you promise after promise and countless scriptural prayers that help you intercede in agreement with his will and purpose for your kids.

Accept God's plan when it is different from yours. Pam had been able to care for her daughter Jan since she was diagnosed with severe cerebral palsy as a baby. But when she was sixteen, doctors recommended she be placed in the Children's Center, a special needs long-term care facility in their city. Pam had prayed to be able to take care of Jan as long as Jan lived. She *never* wanted to put Jan in a residential home. But because of her daughter's critical medical needs and her growing size, Pam could no longer care for her at home. God knew this mom's heart and her limits, and she increasingly began to realize that was why he made provision for Jan to be cared for in a better way than Pam could give. For Pam, accepting that provision brought a leap in faith and peace.

Fear of her daughter's suffering, fear of not being there for her if something happened, fear of the unknown—the only way Pam wasn't overwhelmed by these possibilities was to keep her eyes on God's promises. As she puts it, "When I can't trace God's hand, I can trust his heart."

On those days when Pam saw her daughter suffering and didn't understand, she mirrored God's Word back to him, praying things like: "Jan's times are in your hands . . . let me trust those times to you, Father" (Ps. 31:15) or "Thank you, Father, that you have given your angels charge over Jan to guard her in all her ways" (Ps. 91:11). As she did this, God increased her joy as she learned to trust him one day at a time.

Besides visiting Jan daily at the center, Pam has found tremendous ways to help the other parents of handicapped children there. She also began to work part-time for their church. God further widened her ministry by opening up opportunities to speak to women's groups and write a book about Jan's life. Remember that when you let go of your expectations and are open to what God has planned, he doesn't do less but *more*. More, Ephesians 3:20 says, than you could ever ask, think, or imagine, according to his riches in glory in Christ Jesus.

Provide a prayer cover for your children. Praying for your children helps you put them in God's hands not only in a crisis but in everyday situations as well. Besides your own prayers for them, join with a prayer partner. Two close, faithful prayer partners have been a great source of strength to Dana. One lives 250 miles away, but once a week at 6:15 in the morning they meet by phone for a powerful time of praying together. If possible, link up with another mother who has walked with God as she faced adversity with her children. These mothers really know how to pray for you and your kids!

> When we are careful to instantly let go of all needless worries and restless thoughts . . . then we shall find ourselves on plateaus of peace even in the midst of the straight and narrow.
>
> *Francois Fénelon, Let Go*

Prayer networks are also important when there are ongoing needs or crises—whether it's a prodigal son in harm's way or a child with medical needs like Soren. Dana's local church, her Bible study group, and Moms in Touch group have been part of that network to support Soren in prayer. They also developed an electronic prayer network where they share prayer requests and praises with hundreds of family and friends here and around the world through e-mail. This enabled Dana to send on-the-spot requests from Mayo Clinic and receive wonderful notes of encouragement while walking through some of the most challenging times. Fear is banished and peace fills this mother's heart when she knows others are lifting her son to the Throne of Grace for God's mercy and help. (See www.momsintouch.org for a prayer group nearest you.)

Is it your prodigal teenager that keeps your heart anxious? Never give up on a child in sin. Instead, ask God to give him a hunger for righteousness, take the blinders off so he will see the deception of Satan, and flood him with friends who will influence him positively for Christ. As Jean Fleming says, "Even when it seems God doesn't hear our prayers for our children, we must keep on praying persistently. Prayer may be our most effective ministry in our children's lives."

The Lifeline of God's Word

> All your children shall be taught by the LORD,
> And great shall be the peace of your children.

Isaiah 54:13 NKJV

Lord, I thank you for your promise that you will teach my children and guide them in your ways, and great shall be their—and my—peace.

> For this boy [girl] I prayed, and the LORD has given me my petition which I asked of Him. So I have also dedicated him to the LORD; as long as he lives he is dedicated to the LORD.

1 Samuel 1:27–28 NASB

> Lord, when doubts fill my mind, when my heart is in turmoil, quiet me and give me renewed hope and cheer.

Psalm 94:19 TLB

Lord, just as Hannah dedicated her son Samuel to you, I dedicate and entrust my child into your faithful, loving hands. As long as he lives, Father, he belongs to you and is dedicated to you. When doubts and turmoil fill my mind, quiet my heart and give me renewed hope and cheer.

eight

Overcoming Fears about Finances

My God will meet all your needs according to his glorious
riches in Christ Jesus.

Philippians 4:19

As we rode up the Maine highway, I felt like a fifty-pound
weight was on my shoulders. My friend Linda sang along
with a Christmas tape as she drove the car, but I was preoccupied with my own anxious thoughts. Just then a car passed,
loaded with laughing kids and brightly wrapped packages
crammed into the back windshield.

It's getting so close to Christmas, I thought, *but there's no sign
of Christmas money at our house this year. I don't know how I'm
going to pay our rent, let alone buy the children any gifts. If we could
just skip the holidays . . .*

The car veered toward the craggy, sharp rocks that jutted out on the right side of the highway. I braced against the dashboard and my whole body tensed up.

"Relax," Linda said. "I've driven this road a hundred times. Are you always this nervous in the car?"

"No, not until our car wreck last summer," I answered, staring out the window.

It all came rushing back as the scene flashed on the movie screen of my mind. *The curve, the motorcycle racing around the bend, heading directly toward my car . . . Then swerving to try to miss it. In slow motion horror, the out-of-control motorcycle flew head-on into us, burst into flames, and slid under the van. I was thrown into the dashboard, seat belt broken. Stunned from the impact of the crash, I staggered out of the car and watched helplessly as it burned—knowing insurance wouldn't be enough to replace it.*

That car wreck had become a symbol of every out-of-control thing in my life since our move. Lately I seemed to be worrying constantly about whether we could pay the rent or electric bill.

The situation I faced was anxiety producing, exaggerated by the holiday season. But financial fears affect everyone in every walk of life: The farm couple who fear they'll lose the ranch that has been in the family for three generations. The small businesswoman unable to make payroll. The single mom who has been told her house will be repossessed if she can't make the payment. The college student whose financial aid loans haven't come through and she doesn't know how she can make it through the semester.

If you have experienced fears about finances, you're not alone. In fact, in recent studies showing that women suffer even more anxiety and distress than men, they reveal that a great deal of that stress is related to finances, especially in a tottering economy. A woman raising children alone has particular stresses related to money. Many women fear that they cannot make it financially on their own if their spouse's business fails. They have a hard time believing that God really cares for them.

What can we do when finances look like they're falling apart, when we've worked hard, paid bills, and tried to save, but the rug gets pulled out from under us? That day on the highway when I shared with my friend what was really behind my anxiety was a first step for me. She helped me bring my concerns to God instead of feeling paralyzed and discouraged about them. By getting my fears out of my head into the light of day, things didn't seem so overwhelming. What I realized then is that fear is much like an avalanche. Once the rocks or anxious thoughts start rolling, they are hard to stop, especially by ourselves alone.

> **Worry is like a rocking chair.**
> **It gives you something to do,**
> **but it won't get you anywhere.**
>
> *Anonymous*

Loneliness causes our fears to snowball, I've found, but "friendship divides burdens and multiplies hope," someone once said. I experienced that kind of hope and encouragement as Linda and I talked and prayed together. And as I continued to turn each fearful thought into a prayer, my own perspective began to be transformed. Prayer reminds us that we're never alone, that God is always there ready to help us. While fear keeps us turned into ourselves, wrapped in our own thoughts and burdens, when we turn our fears over to God, he moves our gaze to others around us who need our help.

Although things didn't turn around overnight in our financial situation, a few days later I felt something or Someone nudging me to call the International Student Office of a local university to ask if a student who would otherwise be alone for the holidays might like to join our family. We didn't have much, but by sharing Christmas with a girl from Shanghai who was alone ten thousand miles away from her home, who had never sung a carol or heard the Christmas story, it became one of the richest, most meaningful holidays we had experienced.

Between the invitation to Zhu Hong and Christmas weekend, a couple back home placed an order for some of my books they wanted to give as gifts, and the money I made provided enough for a gift for each person, including our international guest . . . and a turkey dinner. And I also found part-time work as a substitute teacher in the local schools, which alleviated some of our financial strain.

God Is Enough

Single moms have even greater financial pressures and often no one to share them with. When Susan's husband left her and her two young girls, she had no extended family around to help or offer assistance in any way. While some single mothers have parents, relatives, or siblings to give them support, she had no one in the city where they lived.

Susan was a new believer, having accepted Christ shortly after the divorce. One night about a year after the split, she became overwhelmed by grief and guilt feelings about their failed marriage. Added to that load, intense pressures—financial and personal—had piled up and burdened her to the breaking point. It was like the weight of the world was on her shoulders.

Numb from the emotional stress of twelve-hour workdays and trying to handle all the demands of single parenting with little left of herself to give her girls at night, she didn't know if she had the strength to go on. She called a local hospital in desperation, "I feel like I'm having a nervous break-down. I'm anxious. I can't sleep. Can I come in during the middle of the night if I can't make it through alone?" she asked. Just knowing she had someplace to turn for help settled her down a little.

> True faith is never found alone; it is accompanied by expectation.
>
> *C. S. Lewis*

Instead of going to the hospital, however, Susan was led to open her Bible to Isaiah 61 and read that the Lord was sent to heal the brokenhearted, that he could turn her mourning into joy and give her a thankful attitude for her heavy, burdened spirit. As she read the words of that chapter, it was like healing salve over her heart. She realized the strength that was available for her in Christ. She remembered how God had been with her all along, even when she wasn't consciously aware of his presence. And she knew he was right there with her in her lowest moments—he was her husband when there was no one else. That gave Susan the confidence to trust that God would be with her in all the challenges she faced.

Susan's motto became: "When you come to the point where he's all you have, you realize he's all you need." She found God was enough. His Word gave her the energy to persevere, and his Spirit guided her in every decision.

Through that guidance, she left a position in commercial real estate, which took her away from her daughters until after dark every night. She started a housecleaning business, which actually provided more income *and* the flexibility to be home when her girls were off from school. The five-bedroom house they lived in had to be sold but was badly in need of repair. Houses in their area were sitting on the market for one to two years and were selling for $10,000 lower than the asking price, so her house needed to be in top condition in order to sell. Instead of giving in to the "what ifs" . . . what if I can't sell it, what if I can't afford to get it fixed up . . . she and her five-foot-tall cleaning assistant took off two layers of shingles and put on a new roof, laid a new linoleum floor in the kitchen, and painted the whole house inside and out. With those improvements, the house sold for only a little less than the asking price, which enabled her to buy a nice house they could afford. Every step of the process, God was right with her in a protective, strengthening way.

If Susan had depleted her energy with worry and emotional distress, there was no way she could have accomplished what she did. Maybe you have heard of the 3 Ds needed for success— Desire, Discipline, and Determination. For Susan, it was a fourth D that provided the extra adrenalin to press on—*Desperation!*

Embracing Reality

Lynn found that one of the pitfalls of being single was thinking that some man was going to arrive, take care of her, and rescue her from all her financial burdens. But when she sank into that fantasy, it was easy to fall deeper and deeper in debt. Instead, she began to embrace the fact that for the rest of her life she would need to be financially responsible, but she could always depend on God as her source. As she faced the financial area head-on and turned it over to him, her finances became manageable and didn't keep her in a constant state of fear and anxiety.

For her, that came to mean that no matter what happened or how bad things were, if she was faithful to give God his part of her income by tithing, she had peace. Along the way, he has never failed or forsaken her, and she was even able to pay for everything, including graduate school. However, during those grad school years, money was tight. Sometimes she had no idea how she was going to pay for the next semester's tuition. But whenever tuition was due, someone would always hit her old car. It never was her fault—one time a tow truck hit her car while it was parked on the street. The car became more and more battle worn because she used the repair money for tuition instead of at the body shop, but her fees were always paid on time. And when Lynn received her master's degree, she wasn't burdened by thousands of dollars of school debt.

People sent her money anonymously; special projects came up for earning extra income—maybe in the eleventh hour, but needs were always provided for. She was also careful to keep herself on a budget, especially for food since as a single who didn't like to cook for one, it was easy to go out to eat too often and run up her credit card bill!

God Our Provider

How could Denise, a mother of five children, cope when their family business abruptly halted? The fifteen-year-old business provided stage technicians, lighting, and labor for concerts in the city's main entertainment arena. Winters had always been a struggle because it was the slow season for concerts. But at 5:30 on a December Friday evening, they found out their entire contract for the year was canceled. Grocery money to feed their family of seven dwindled rapidly. Rent was due in a few days, and there was not enough money in their checking account to cover it. What kept Denise from dissolving in fear and despair?

"I've learned that the God who led the Israelites through the Red Sea is the same God who will provide and open up work for us," Denise told me. "He hasn't changed just because we've lost our job." Denise survived and thrived by exchanging worry for wonder.

Regardless of the balance in their checking account, Denise can get up each morning with a sense of anticipation and gratefulness because she knows God has a plan and he has cared for them through lean times in the past. Like the day a bread truck stopped in front of their house, and the bread man asked, "Could you use some bread? I've got a lot left over today and I've finished my route. Take whatever you want." Or the time a friend needed home school books and Denise was able to sell some used ones to her that day. Or the time a neighbor down the road prayed for their family, then called saying they had an extra $250 in their savings account they wanted to give them.

> It seems to be God's plan to allow all sorts of things to happen that would naturally cause fear, but to forestall them by the assurance of His presence.
>
> *Amy Carmichael*

Learning to "wonder" instead of worry has not been without challenge. Shortly after losing their yearly contract, they had to move out of their house because they couldn't afford the rent. However, they were able to find a large trailer home that actually met their needs better. Denise found part-time work cleaning houses with a friend, and her husband found a temporary job.

The joy and excitement in their hearts is something only God can give as they live with a sense that he is their provider. A house, car, or job couldn't give that kind of joy, and those things won't remain. But God is going to be there no matter what.

From Fear to Faith

Maybe you experienced fear when you signed the contract for your first home. Maybe instead of celebrating, you began to fear that you wouldn't have enough to make those monthly payments. Perhaps you never gave finances a thought until your husband was laid off from his job along with one thousand other people in his high-tech company. Or your anxieties snowballed when creditors started calling or when you realized your kids were only a few years away from college and your savings had been eaten up. Regardless of what the situation is that triggers your fear, here are practical ways to move toward faith when anxiety about finances grips your heart.

> **Faith is . . .**
> **Confidence in God**
> **When money is running out,**
> **Not rolling in.**
>
> *Pamela Reeve, Faith Is . . .*

Review who God is and write down his goodness toward you. Write in your journal all the ways God has provided in the past. Include little and big blessings he has given and answered prayers. Write down things you know about God and ways you have experienced his nature and lovingkindness through everyday joys and gifts you've received. It can change your fear to faith, just as it did for Carol when the bottom dropped out. Her world was shaken when her husband's partnership dissolved and his health deteriorated, causing their income to plummet. Any sense of security Carol had was suddenly vaporized.

She was frightened by their financial situation, worried about her husband, and afraid their house would have to be sold. For a while she just survived day to day in a fog. But when she started reviewing what she had learned about God's nature so far and read what she had recorded in her journal aloud, she discovered three truths to cling to that turned her panic to peace: *God is faithful; God is good; God loves me.*

Carol also began keeping a "Glory Journal." Looking for the good things that happened each day, no matter what difficulties she faced, Carol listed them in a notebook: the gorgeous colors of fall leaves that blew in the yard, the progress her son made in math class, the loving care of a friend who brought her family a casserole. The Glory Journal kept her focus on the positive and helped her avoid sliding into an abyss of negativity, discouragement, and fear.

Don't put things off—procrastination causes more anxiety. If debts are piling up because income is low, don't run from creditors, which will only make the situation worse and escalate your fears. Run toward them but get help! Fear can cause you to procrastinate paying your bills because you're afraid there won't be enough in the bank to cover them. Seek financial counseling from a reliable accountant or a reputable credit counseling service. Read books from Christian financial experts like Larry Burkett, Ron Blue, and Mary Hunt. Mary, who once had over $100,000 in unsecured debt herself, is founder of *Cheapskate Monthly.* She offers a wealth of wise advice on getting out of debt and in the process living within your means (see her web site CheapskateMonthly.com).

Go about the business God has given you to do. For most of us, that's a full plate of responsibilities. Do the next thing, and your fears will begin to dissipate. When you focus on the tasks at hand and do them as service to God, you don't have as much time to worry about what's going to happen. If you're not sure what to do, ask God, "What's my part in this? What am I supposed to do?" and get some wise counsel to help you gain insight on that.

Even if things get tough, if you follow God's principles of handling money, you can experience peace and provision. When my friend Cynthia's husband, Dave, lost his job, they purposed to keep following biblical principles of money management they had learned from Larry Burkett's ministry, including a commitment to not incur any more debt—not even to replace their old car or put their children through college. For her, the "fight of faith" was to keep believing and following what God said they were to do with their money (giving and avoiding borrowing, for example) instead of jumping ship and doing things their own way.

What helped Cynthia the most when she began to worry about how they would pay the bills during those lean times was to run the worst scenario through in her mind and think, *What is the worst that can happen?* Then she asked herself, *Is God able?*

She decided that even if they lost their house and ate bread and water for a while, the peace God gives when they believe his promises and manage money his way was worth more than *things,* than a big car or vacation. That peace comes not by having everything they want but by living simply and following biblical principles of finance. She realized and believed that while we can never command God to do what we want, if we're managing money his way, then when crisis comes, we have a strong foundation, and things don't get chaotic.

In facing her fears this way, she finds herself energized to wait on God, to do her part, and to see how he guides and what he does. Their family of six never missed any meals—she's the best cook I know! They not only had enough to feed their own children but to offer hospitality and warm meals to countless people they've invited into their home over the years.

Personalize the promises of Scripture and fear will flee. When you are tempted to speak anxiously about your financial situation, exchange your fearful thoughts for the truth and focus on what God says in his Word. Instead of saying, "We'll never have enough; things are just getting worse," affirm: "We have everything we need to live a life that pleases God. It was all given to us by God's own power when we learned that he had invited us to share in his wonderful goodness!" (See 2 Peter 1:3.)

Adding to your Peace Packet verses that specifically apply to money matters and God's provision can help you face challenging financial times:

So do not worry, saying, "What shall we eat?" or "What shall we drink?" or "What shall we wear?" For the pagans run after all these things, and your heavenly Father knows that you need them. But seek first his kingdom and his righteousness, and all these things will be given to you as well. Therefore do not worry about tomorrow . . .

Matthew 6:31–34

I was young and now I am old,
yet I have never seen the righteous forsaken
or their children begging bread.

Psalm 37:25

Give, and it will be given to you. A good measure, pressed down, shaken together and running over, will be poured into your lap. For with the measure you use, it will be measured to you.

Luke 6:38

The young lions do lack and suffer hunger;
But they who seek the LORD shall not be in want of any
good thing.

Psalm 34:10 NASB

Write each verse on a 3x5 card and carry the cards with you. If you start worrying, get them out and review them. As you meditate on God's promises daily, say the verse in your own words, telling God you are depending on him. Then continue to add promises from your own Bible reading that build your confidence in God and his ability to provide.

Share the burdens. Even those who have wealth aren't always exempt from fears about finances. Nationally known financial consultant Ron Blue said recently that prosperity leads to fear of loss, and fear of loss leads to loss of faith. Whatever your anxieties or concerns are about finances, give them to God one by one and be specific about your needs. Talk and pray about these heavy burdens with a friend. If anxious thoughts about your financial situation resurface, which they often do, give them back to God right then. Release them as many times as necessary until your mind is free from fretting about them.

Don't be like the little boy who took his broken bicycle to the repair shop to be fixed. The repairman assured him it would be as good as new and told him to leave his bike in the repair room. The repairman promised to call when he was finished fixing it. But after being home for a day or two, the boy began to worry about his bike: *Can the repairman really fix the problem? Is he going to call me or lose my bike? Why isn't it ready yet?* Before he knew it, the little boy raced down to the shop and reclaimed his bicycle—still broken.

You and I are much like that little boy. We may give our financial problem to God, but moments or hours later, we take it back— and start handling it ourselves. If you find you've reclaimed your

"broken bike," or broken money matters, give them back to God
. . . and leave them there!

The Lifeline of God's Word

The Lord is my shepherd, I shall not be in want.

Psalm 23:1

*Lord, you are my shepherd. You give me everything I need so I
won't be in want.*

Remember this: Whoever sows sparingly will also reap sparingly, and whoever sows generously will also reap generously.
Each man should give what he has decided in his heart to
give, not reluctantly or under compulsion, for God loves a
cheerful giver. And God is able to make all grace abound to
you, so that in all things at all times, having all that you need,
you will abound in every good work.

2 Corinthians 9:6–8

*Lord, thank you for making all grace abound to me, so that in all
things at all times, having all that I need, I will abound in every good
work. Help me to be a cheerful giver and follow your ways of handling
whatever money or resources are entrusted to me. Empower me to sow
generously and reap generously and to always give you the praise from
a thankful heart for all you have provided and blessed me with.*

Now to him who is able to do immeasurably more than all
we ask or imagine, according to his power that is at work
within us, to him be glory in the church and in Christ Jesus
throughout all generations, for ever and ever!

Ephesians 3:20–21

*Father, help me remember that you are able to do immeasurably
more than all I could ask or imagine, according to your mighty
power at work within me. To you be glory forever and ever!*

nine

Overcoming Fears That Harm Relationships

There is no fear in love. But perfect love drives out fear, because fear has to do with punishment. The one who fears is not made perfect in love. We love because he first loved us.

1 John 4:18–19

When you can't trust God, it's hard to trust anyone else, especially your husband. And that lack of trust can damage relationships. I found this out by personal experience. In fact, my anxiety threatened to ruin our first Christmas together. Holmes and I were on our way back from Wellington, Kansas, to Dallas for a New Year's Eve celebration of my mother's birthday. It was December 1969, and we had only been married one month. Little did Holmes know the basket case of nerves he would have sitting beside him in the car.

Since almost everyone in my family had a touch of "car phobia," I thought it normal the way my big sister threw her arms on the dashboard when she thought I was stopping too close to the car in front of us. It seemed natural that we were all such experts at backseat driving. After all, the whole family had been on the fateful trip to Ruidosa, New Mexico, when my sister Georgia fell asleep leaning on the car door and went flying out of the car on the highway when the door inadvertently opened. Mama, with me in her arms, became hysterical and ran back to get her. Papa, normally reserved, was shaken as he scooped my bloody, unconscious sister up in his arms. He declared that we'd never take another family trip— and we didn't, as long as he lived. Georgia survived with only abrasions from head to foot; but car phobia was the long-term effect for our whole family.

> It is the law of the spiritual life that every act of trust makes the next act less difficult, until at length, if these acts are persisted in, trusting becomes, like breathing, the natural unconscious action of the redeemed soul.
>
> *Hannah Whitall Smith*

As the first snowflakes were beginning to fall, Holmes and I drove away from his grandparents' house, waving, smiling and excited about getting back to Dallas and our little duplex in Waco. It was our first New Year's Eve as a married couple. Having grown up in Dallas where we saw snow only once in about every five years, I loved the way the Kansas countryside looked as we drove by the wheat fields now growing whiter and whiter. But my delight turned to fear as the snow blanketed the road and the highway grew slicker.

Holmes felt confident about driving us back to Texas safely; he'd had lots of experience driving on snow and ice while growing up in northern Oklahoma. Besides, to him this was a great adventure, and he loved adventures. However, I was petrified when daylight turned to darkness and we began sliding on the icy roads. Miss White-Knuckle-Door-Handle Hugger clung to it as if somehow gripping it could save me.

"Holmes, please slow down!" I said, fear rising up and choking me.

"I'm only going twenty-five miles per hour," he answered. "Relax."

Relax! I thought. This looked like a full-scale blizzard to me, and we could barely see anything ahead for the whirlwind of white covering the windshield. There was *no way* I could relax. My foot "braked" to slow us down, but that didn't work. It felt like we were going too fast. But even five miles per hour would have been too fast for me. I was so scared I could barely speak except to say an occasional, "Slow down!"

Holmes ignored me and kept driving steadily along. As we cruised through several small towns, snow drifted in huge piles. Only one lane was open. Cars were careening off the road because under the snow was a solid sheet of ice. But whenever we slid off to one side of the road, Holmes somehow got us back on and kept going.

"Holmes, why don't we just stop?"

"We don't have the option of stopping. We're between towns and it's too cold to pull to the side of the road. Besides, we'd freeze."

"Then let's spend the night in the next little town and continue driving in the morning when the roads are better." As soon as we slid into the next town, we passed several motels, but they all had "No Vacancy" signs out. My spirits fell.

"Look! There's a sign saying travelers can stay at the high school gymnasium overnight because of the snowstorm," I said, thinking that was a great idea.

"Your family is expecting us for your mom and sister's birthday party, and I'm not about to sleep on a cold, hard gym floor tonight."

As much as I loved a family party, sleeping on a gym floor sounded better to me than six to eight more hours of this stressful driving. And the line of cars turning into the school ahead of us agreed. I pleaded to join them.

"There's no reason to stop," Holmes bristled. "We're fine; I'll get us to Dallas safely."

With each mile Holmes grew more irritated by my nervousness. I felt hurt because he didn't understand my fear. He didn't appreciate my backseat driving. He didn't feel affirmed since I wasn't admiring his driving skills. I was upset that he wouldn't drive more slowly. He thought he *was* driving carefully and felt criticized. Anger, fear, and hurt welled up in me and neither of us could relate to the other.

When we finally arrived at my parents' home in Dallas well after midnight that New Year's Eve, I was worn out from the stressful drive, even though I hadn't done any of the driving. (As I have shared before fear will do that to you—drain all your energy.) Holmes and I were barely speaking. Unfortunately, this was a scene that occurred several times throughout the early years of our marriage. Some of the worst times between the normally peace-loving, low-conflict two of us were in the car.

God Intervenes

I don't know where we'd have ended up if God hadn't intervened in our marriage, because my fears (plus all our other baggage) were putting a big strain on the relationship. One of the wonderful things about God is that he knows all about us and loves us anyway. He knows our needs even before we ask and knows what is underneath the weaknesses when we are clueless. And when we let him, God can marvelously transform our fears and heal our hurts.

As Holmes and I grew in Christ, we gradually gave God more and more of our lives: habits, finances, careers. We told the Lord we'd go any direction he wanted, and he opened up new doors for Holmes. He was so faithful in these other areas that we gave him our marriage too. We knew we needed his help and healing. After all, in eight years of trying to do life on our own, a lot of resentment and negative patterns built up. But since we couldn't afford counseling, we had no idea how God could bring about change.

In 1978 Holmes and I attended a weekend conference that focused on restoration of the family, church, and nation. We were inspired by hearing Peter Marshall speak, and on Sunday a healing service was planned. Although we'd never heard of a healing service, it sounded like a good idea. Despite all efforts with medication, allergy shots, and diet changes, our son's asthma was still a struggle, so this invitation to have someone pray for him sounded great.

On Sunday afternoon we sat with our children at the back of the auditorium with several hundred other people to hear the message. Then we were instructed to write our prayer request on paper provided in the bulletin and come up to one of the three ministers to be prayed for.

After a wise, older pastor shared about what the Bible had to say about healing, I thought he looked like the best person.

> Let faith always speak against feeling. When feeling says, "In myself I am sinful, I am dark, I am weak, I am poor, I am sad," let faith say, "In Christ I am holy, I am light, I am strong, I am rich, I am joyful."
>
> *Andrew Murray*

So I wrote, "Our son has severe asthma and chronic allergies that have caused trips to the ER and hospital since he was four. Could you pray for him?" We hesitantly got in that pastor's line. However, his line was so long that we were steered over to Peter Marshall.

We sat down on the pew before him when it was our turn for prayer. Reverend Marshall didn't know us, but he looked intently down the row at each of us and at our son. Then he looked back at me and said, *"You're* the one who really needs prayer. Come up and let me pray for you."

But you don't understand, I thought. *It's not me—it's our son who needs prayer for his asthma. That's what we came for.* Not one to argue with the person in charge, I walked up with my family and Reverend Marshall began.

"Lord, heal the heart of this young woman who lost her father as a child. Take away her sense of being abandoned by her father and you . . ." he began to pray with an understanding only God's Spirit could have given him. I hadn't written anything about my past on the sheet. Somehow God gave this man who had lost his own father when he was ten years old the knowledge that losing my father when I was a child left me with a sense of being abandoned, resulting in a lack of trust (in my husband, in God, in any man) and many fears. He prayed with compassion for God to heal all those emotions and to show me how faithful my heavenly Father is, how he had led me and protected me all through my life. He asked that trust be rebuilt between me and my husband. As he prayed, it was like the deep root system of fear and distrust was literally pulled out of my soul.

And as he continued praying, my reserved husband began to weep uncontrollably, the hurt literally pouring out of him for my never trusting him to drive safely enough or handle decisions or anything else. I'd never seen Holmes cry like this in our whole marriage. Resentment and irritations were washed from both of us as the tears flowed. Peter continued praying for our marriage to be healed and for us to truly "cleave" to one another and become one.

At the close of the weekend we stood with other couples to renew our vows, feeling like the old passed away and we had a brand-new start to our relationship. And although our son was not prayed for as I had planned, his asthma did begin to improve. I got a new glimpse of the Lord that day and was filled with awe that he who was in charge of the whole universe was so caring that he would send a man like Peter Marshall from across the country, a man whose father had died when he was a child, just as mine had, to minister to the deepest part of my heart and bring freedom.

Fear Hinders Relationships

Like me, many women today fear trusting a man. Because the divorce rate is over 50 percent, many women were raised without fathers. Some feel they can't depend on a man or commit to a relationship. But according to Barbara Sullivan in *The Control Trap*,

> Today's widespread fear of trusting men can actually become the catalyst that causes us to place our trust and faith in God.

The stress that comes when we attempt to be in control of relationships will ultimately rob us of the joy of life. We can become free of that stress when we release our control to God and begin to live in freedom from fear.[1]

Maybe your fear isn't a lack of trust in a person like I experienced but a fear of being abandoned or rejected. That kind of fear usually causes a woman to build walls around her heart, and in the process she grows lonelier and lonelier. Or fear of rejection may lead her to people pleasing and being taken advantage of by friends and family. "One of my biggest fears is investing time and heart in a friendship and then seeing my female friend marry and move away," says one single woman. "It has happened over and over and I come up empty." Some fear being used, being betrayed, being alone, or not measuring up to what others think they should be.

One of the main places a fear of rejection comes from is our early family experiences. As Stephen Arterburn and Dr. Paul Meier say,

> Parents are of supreme importance to all of us as children. We desperately need our parents' love and want to know we mean the world to Mom *and* Dad. When unconditional love isn't possible, the door opens to a deeply unsettling fear our parents may be about to jettison us out of their lives. Such fear of rejection is terrifying![2]

Ever since she was a little girl, Stephanie had struggled with this kind of rejection. Her father would say over and over to her and her sister, "Nobody loves you like your daddy," but he was the one who forgot to pick her up from school in the first grade . . . ignored her birthdays . . . wasn't at the airport when she flew home to visit him in high school, and had his girlfriends about four years older than she was escort her to the mall when it was his court-ordered visitation day.

Not having a relationship with her dad left a hole in Stephanie's heart, and she carried a yearning for a father figure into adulthood. It also caused her to unconsciously pick a "substitute for the rejecting parent,"[3] first a handsome guy who turned out to be a drug addict, and two years later, a knight in shining armor who swept her off her feet, but once married he turned into a nightmare who mentally, physically, and sexually abused her. After fourteen months, that marriage was over.

> Maybe you have been looking for a long time for that promised peace of God that passes all understanding (Phil. 4:7). Today, it can radiantly transform you as you allow the stubble of mistrust to be consumed in the fire of His great love for you, through which no eternal harm can ever come.
>
> *Barbara Sullivan,* The Control Trap

Still she kept praying daily that God would send her someone to love.

Folding laundry one Saturday afternoon, she lamented over her marital situation. Her emotions over the past year had run the gamut from rage, abandonment, fear, and sorrow to hopelessness. She began to blame her suffering on God. Crying uncontrollably, she fell to her knees. *Why did you do this to me? Why? Why, God?*

"You prayed for someone you could love," was the reply of the Almighty as she heard him whisper to her heart. All of a sudden, the tears stopped. She had thought romantic love was the answer, the solution to the emptiness in her life. It was as though God said, "You asked me to show you how to love . . . I am giving you more than this man . . . I am teaching you to love me." She realized then that unfortunately there had been no room in her heart for God until her heart was broken by a mortal man. Slowly she began to learn to love God, who always returns her love and never breaks her heart. As the old fears of rejection, abandonment, and loss were healed, a place was eventually made for a healthy relationship with a godly, loving man, her darling husband, Michael.

Instead of looking for love in all the wrong places as Stephanie did, other people cope with fear of rejection by withdrawing and retreating from any attempt to love or be loved. "We seek safety in going unnoticed. We reach out to no one lest we be rebuffed. Jesus commanded the disciples to 'love one another as I have loved you' (John 15:12 NKJV). Shyness utterly stifles the ability to do that and, in that sense, could be considered a sin," said Bruce Larson in *Living beyond Our Fears: Discovering Life When You're Scared to Death.*[4]

From Fear to Faith

Instead of withdrawing, substituting, retreating, or letting our fears harm our relationships, we can let these struggles drive us to the cross. For as Larson says, "Fear is the handle by which we lay hold of God."[5] Laying hold of God enables us to receive his love for us—an unfailing, unconditional, powerful love that drives out the fear of rejection and enables us to be vessels of love to others.

Experience God's love. As the little verse goes, "Do you love me, or do you not? You told me once, but I forgot." Many of us have heard a lot about God's love. We've read about his love and seen his love in other people's lives. But have we experienced God's love in a way that brings our hearts to rest?

One Sunday just as we were singing the words, "There's no place I'd rather be than in your arms of love, in your arms of love, holding me still, holding me near in your arms of love,"[6] I noticed Bonnie, a third grader I taught in Children's Church, going up and down the aisles, looking for her dad. Bonnie had a bewildered look on her face as she passed each row, but she was persistently looking up and down each aisle until she found him.

Finally she arrived at our aisle and saw her daddy a few seats down from me. She took off, climbing around me and several others. She literally leaped up in his arms and rested her head on her father's shoulder. As the song continued, he held her small hand in his, and the biggest smile I've ever seen lit up her face. She was home! This picture of what we were singing struck me: God wants our hearts to come home to him—he wants us to feel that same kind of daddy love from him as Bonnie did from her dad, only much more.

First John 4:18 tells us that we don't have to fear someone who loves us perfectly as God does. Or as the Message translation puts it, "There is no room in love for fear. Well-formed love banishes fear." Knowing his complete and total love for us delivers us from any dread or worry of what he might do to us or what life would deal us. It frees us from having to please people or from being afraid they'll reject us or abandon us—frees us to truly love.

David knew what it was like to be misunderstood by friends and family and pursued by enemies who betrayed him. But despite rejection and discouragement, he proclaimed, "No one whose hope is in you will ever be put to shame" (Ps. 25:3). No matter what people did or how they treated him, his hope was in the Lord.

This leads us to a much greater, more eternal reason to know God than just living a life free of fear. Knowing God through trusting our lives to the lordship of Jesus Christ is an end in itself. In fact, it is the end, the purpose for which we were created, as the ancient tradition of the Westminster Catechism states: "The chief end of man is to glorify God and to enjoy Him forever."

As A. W. Tozer said, "God is not asking you to come to Christ just to attain peace of mind or to make you a better businessman or woman. You were created to worship. God wants you to know His redemption so you will desire to worship and praise Him."[7] What a great invitation. If you don't know God, take time to ask Christ to forgive your sins, to reveal himself to you and come into your heart, and to fit you for heaven so you will live with him forever.

Verbally share your fear with someone else. When you confess what you are afraid of, whether that is "I don't know if I'll ever get married," or "I'm afraid I won't ever have a close friend again," your fear shrinks to a manageable size and solutions begin to come into view. You may need professional help to discover why you are afraid of people or why you fear rejection. But little by little you will gain insight into the roots of your fear as you talk them over with a counselor or a trusted mentor.

When you hide the fear inside your head and heart, it multiples and isolates you from other people. When you acknowledge instead of deny or cover up your fear with some self-defeating strategy, it can propel you into pursuing God and healthy relationships. Don't let your fears keep you away from connecting with others in a small group, a Bible study, or the loving community of a church. Open yourself up to God's power by asking for prayer, because the Lord can sometimes do more healing through just moments spent in prayer with one of his faithful servants, as he did through Peter Marshall's intercession for me, than is accomplished through months of therapy.

Look to God's Word to discover who you are in Christ. The misbeliefs we hold about ourselves are at the heart of our fear of rejection. Go to God's love letter to you, the Bible, and exchange every misbelief or lie about yourself with the truth about who you are in Christ. Overrule what you think or feel with what is true about you according to Scripture. If you tend to think that you are unworthy and unacceptable, replace that misbelief with God's Word, which says that in Christ, you are accepted and worthy: "I am fearfully and wonderfully made; your works are wonderful, I know that full well" (Ps. 139:14). In saying this, we don't praise ourselves—we praise God for how he made us. We don't boast in ourselves but in the Lord who created us, redeemed us, and has a purpose for us.

When you feel that there is nothing special about you, remember that God says you have been chosen and set apart by him. Not because you are so great without him (actually we are nothing without him) but because you belong to him: "It is because of him that you are in Christ Jesus, who has become for us wisdom from God—that is, our righteousness, holiness and redemption" (1 Cor. 1:30). (Also see Eph. 1:4; Heb. 10:10, 14.) As Leslie Vernick says, "Part of building a proper picture of ourselves is to see ourselves truthfully, as much loved sinners, not as wonderful persons." Romans 5:8 says, "God demonstrates his own love for us in this: While we were still sinners, Christ died for us."

When you think, *I am unwanted* or, *I don't belong to anyone,* review the truth that you have been adopted by God himself and you are his child (Rom. 8:16–17; Gal. 4:5; 1 John 3:2). As you focus your mind on the truth, a confident sense of "Christ-consciousness" will replace your self-consciousness and you will be freer to love others, love God, and love yourself.[8]

No matter what you fear, God's Word has power to set you free. A few years after that healing weekend, we were driving late at night through western Oklahoma when suddenly, out of nowhere, a blinding white mass of snow flying horizontally covered our windshield (and this was April!). We couldn't see the stripes on the two-lane road or even the side of the road because of the blizzard surrounding us. That old fear began rising within me, so I suggested that Holmes slow down, pull over, and stop until the blizzard passed. My hand gripped the armrest, hoping for some semblance of control. At first he was prickly, and then he grew more irritated with my anxiety.

But this time I knew what to do with my fear. I went right to God and began to pray, "Lord, please help me with this. I know your perfect love casts out all fear, so I ask that you would fill me to overflowing with your perfect love so I can somehow relax and not drive my husband crazy as he makes his way through the storm. Help, Lord!"

As I continued to ask for God's help, a song began to bubble up in my consciousness, with the most peaceful melody. "When I am afraid, I will trust in thee," the words played in my mind. "In God whose Word I praise; In God I have put my trust. I shall not be afraid, no, I shall not be afraid!"

Over and over I sang this tune, first in my head and then quietly, aloud. As I sang these words, my fear got smaller and smaller. The anxiety literally shrank before me, and I grew more calm and relaxed. My faith in God's ability and Holmes's driving also increased. My hand relaxed its grip on the armrest, and a sense of humor returned to both of us as we eventually drove out of the blizzard and into New Mexico on our way to our first ski trip.

I've never forgotten the melody God gave me in those moments during the highway blizzard. And the words, I later found when I got to our destination and could look in my Bible, were from Psalm 56:3–4 almost word for word, a passage I had studied a few months before. The Holy Spirit has brought his Word to my mind at other times when I might tend to be afraid too, when I needed to remember in whom I had put my trust. They are just as true today. God and his Word never fail.

Combat the fear of rejection or loneliness by becoming an encourager. Like Barnabas, one of my favorite New Testament heroes, we can become an encourager of others. As Hebrews states: "Let us consider how we may spur one another on toward love and good deeds. Let us not give up meeting together, as some are in the habit of doing, but let us encourage one another—and all the more as you see the Day approaching" (Heb. 10:24–25).

When you set your focus on giving the gift of encouragement by showing appreciation for others, writing a note of thanks, and delivering help, support, hope, kindness, reassurance, and faith to others (for that's what the word *encouragement* means), loneliness begins to flee and your heart, having given much, receives much.

The Lifeline of God's Word

God is love, and all who live in love live in God, and God lives in them. And as we live in God, our love grows more perfect. So we will not be afraid on the day of judgment, but we can face him with confidence because we are like Christ here in this world.

Such love has no fear because perfect love expels all fear. . . . We love each other as a result of his loving us first.

1 John 4:16–19 NLT

Lord, thank you for loving me first so I could know you. Here are the fears I have concerning relationships: _____
I give them all to you. I want your love to be the anchor of my relationships and my life. Help me to live and abide in you, and help your perfect love to cast out all fear from my heart, my emotions, and my mind. Then empower me to love other people as a result of your love living in me.

When I am afraid
I will put my trust in You.

In God, whose word I praise,
In God I have put my trust;
I shall not be afraid.

Psalm 56:3–4 NASB

Father God, when I am afraid, I make the choice and set my will to trust in you and your Word. I praise you for your Word that strengthens me and frees me from fear of what others might do to me. I praise you for your faithfulness that assures me you are always with me. No matter what enemies surround me, I don't have to be afraid. I can walk in your presence, in your life-giving light! Thank you, Lord!

ten

Overcoming a Fear of Flying

O Shepherd, you said you would make my feet like hinds'
feet and set me upon mine High Places.

Hannah Hurnard

We had just boarded our flight from St. Louis to Panama City,
Florida. As the plane rose in the air, my husband and I settled in and began to read our magazines. Then I noticed
the young woman across the aisle. She gripped the armrest as if
it was her lifesaver, gritted her teeth as one does in the dentist
chair before a root canal, and had a look of terror on her face.
The fact that her burly military husband and several family members were sitting around her didn't seem to be quelling her fears.
The flight attendant's reassurance didn't help. And even when
the plane smoothed out and beverages began to be served, there
was no relaxing for Maria. She was still on alert.

Maria isn't alone. Since the hijackings of the airplanes on September 11, 2001, thousands of Americans have been anxious about flying. A month after the attacks, 10 percent of the public had canceled their airline reservations—which doesn't sound like much but represents as many as 19 million airline passengers. And while as time passed more people came back on board the jets, enough people drove or avoided flying by going a different way that several airlines faced bankruptcies. Even before 9-11, research showed that about 25 million Americans were so scared of flying that they wouldn't even board an airplane. And another 30 million were "anxious fliers," who fly because of their jobs or emergencies but are very uncomfortable aloft. That seemed to be the category Maria was in.

> **Do the thing you fear most and the death of fear is certain.**
>
> *Viktor Frankl*

"You seem really nervous," I said to Maria. "Are you doing okay?"

"No, I'm scared to death; I feel like I'm going to throw up," she replied. "But I had to fly. It was my husband's graduation from officer candidate school in the Air Force, we live two thousand miles away, and he expected me to be there." After a few minutes, she asked me, "How can you look so calm?"

"Actually, I used to be afraid of flying too," I explained. I described how whenever a plane took off, I thought about how this could be my last flight, how my family could divide up my small possessions, and I wondered who would take care of our children. My clammy hands gripped the armrest as if I could steer the plane, much like Maria's were doing, and my appetite plummeted with the falling sensation in my stomach on takeoff.

But all that changed when my mom was going through cancer treatment in Las Vegas, of all places. Instead of the alternative treatment helping, the cancer had spread to her brain. Her newest grandbaby, Zachary, her only son George's first child, had just been born in Dallas. And she wanted to see that precious grandson and hold him in her arms more than anything else in the whole world.

However, Mom's physicians would not release her from the hospital to be driven back across the hundreds of miles to Texas because it was too long a journey, one they felt she was too weak to make. Flying her home was the only possibility, they said, but even that risk was too great. Because of brain swelling, increased air pressure could cause her death, so they refused to approve her flight. But she wanted to see that new grandbaby so badly.

This would be a huge dilemma for anyone but especially for my mother, who had had a deeply entrenched fear of flying for years. Riding in a car could induce anxiety, but a plane ride was out of the question. "I have too many dependents," she used to say, referring to myself and my five siblings. But the major event that clipped Mama's wings was a terrific offshore storm she encountered while on a plane en route from Florida to Dallas. Up there twenty-five thousand feet in the sky with the wind whipping the plane around, the rain beating on the windows, and her stomach in her throat, Mom promised God she would never fly again if only he would get her down on the ground safely. And she had kept her promise until now.

That night as she was agonizing about what to do, a local minister had stopped by to visit her in her hospital room—prompted by a friend who phoned from Texas. After the usual hospital pleasantries, the elderly pastor and Mom began to talk. She told him all the things she had hoped to do before she died: She wanted to share about God's goodness in her church in East Texas. She hoped to see some more sunrises on her beloved East Texas ranch and wanted us all to gather there for one last weekend of fun. She wanted to hand out her jewelry and little treasures to her daughters. And most of all, she wanted to hold her new grandson.

Not that Mom feared the end of this life. She hated to leave her children and grandchildren but saw it as a homecoming, a graduation. What she was worried about, she told the pastor, was the timing and how long she had left because she had so much to do to get her "house" in order.

The silver-haired pastor began to read Psalm 139 to Mom: "O LORD, you have searched me and you know me. You know when I sit and when I rise; you perceive my thoughts from afar."

Then he stopped at verse 16: "All the days ordained for me were written in your book before one of them came to be."

Suddenly, as Mama heard those verses read aloud, the truth of God's Word moved from her head deep into her heart. She didn't have to worry about how many days she had left, because they were already written in his book. In fact, those words set Mom free to check herself out of the hospital the next morning, be wheeled in a wheelchair to a jet, and have the most glorious flight of her life into a brilliant purple glow of the Texas sunset to a great homecoming in the DFW terminal. It gave her the chance to hold her new grandson, baby Zachary, in her arms and hug her beloved six children, twenty-two grandchildren, and friends . . . and also to celebrate every day she had left on this earth as a gift from the God who had planned and ordained each one of the days throughout her whole life.

Through seeing Mom freed from her fear of flying and her anxiety about "how many days," the truth of Psalm 139 also deepened in my own life. I came to rest in a sense of God's amazing sovereignty—whether on the ground or in the air, whether flying on a jumbo jet across the country after 9-11 to a speaking engagement or on a little prop plane into the snow-covered mountains of Wyoming to do a parent event.

As I finished my story, Maria asked, "Where were those verses you were talking about?" I got out my Bible and read them to her. And a short time later, right before the plane landed, I felt nudged to ask her, "Could I pray for you concerning your fear?"

"Please do," she responded. As I finished my prayer, I thought how kind of God that he put me right next to someone who suffered a fear I had struggled with. And how wise that he had put me in the sky time after time over the years as I flew to speaking engagements, often enough to face my fears and to learn to enjoy flying. All those flying opportunities gave me a chance to become "desensitized" as the experts call it, because when we face our fears head-on and do the thing we fear instead of shrinking from it, the fears usually diminish.

Virtual Reality

A medical care program in California has successfully used this method—with a high-tech twist—to treat patients suffering from a fear of heights (acrophobia). The principle isn't new; it's just a modern version of facing and confronting one's fears, a technique that has been effectively treating phobias since the sixties.

In order to diminish an irrational fear of snakes, for example, the therapists had the patient confront snakes—from looking at pictures and handling stuffed or toy snakes to actually touching a living but harmless reptile. Although this sounds like cruel and unusual punishment to me, by facing their fears and practicing dealing with whatever it is they are afraid of, the patients' anxieties begin to dissolve.

In contrast, if you avoid everything you are afraid of, the fear *escalates*. Anxiety feeds on itself. Then you begin to fear the feeling of fear: "I don't want to fly because I can't stand that awful feeling of fear I get when I'm in an airplane. I don't want to go to the mall because I'm afraid I'll have a panic attack." Fears graduate in size to the point of agoraphobia—those who are so fearful that they won't leave their own houses.

The psychologist in this new program helped his acrophobic patients face and overcome their fears by using virtual reality, a futuristic technology in which he equipped each person with a virtual reality helmet and a joystick. Then via an interactive, computer-generated environment, they were confronted with heights—in this case, a walk across the Golden Gate Bridge—without ever leaving the safety of the doctor's office. The anxious subjects shook, teetered, and even cried as they inched across the bridge, while the psychologist instructed them to focus on their breathing and muscle tension. After just one hour of virtual reality heights, the patients made significant progress in overcoming their fear of high places.

Unfortunately, due to the expense, not everyone who is afraid of something can take advantage of such high-tech therapy. But we have something even more effective to help us overcome our fears: God's grace and "the utter extravagance of his work in us who trust him—endless energy, boundless strength!" (Eph. 1:18 MESSAGE). With the surpassing greatness of his power in us, we can face what we fear, confront it, and see our anxiety shrink before our eyes.

Thus one of God's best methods of recovery is to give us chance after chance to do the very thing we'd like to avoid. It works for many types of anxiety. As Dale Carnegie once said, the chief cause of people's fear of public speaking is simply that they are not accustomed to speaking in public. Therefore, a routine part of his famous course is weekly public speaking for all participants. Practice, practice, practice in the fearful situation. The result? The participants' fears diminished.

I Want off This Plane!

Maria, my mother, and I aren't the only women who were a little hesitant about a plane ride. Melanie, a cardiac care nurse, could identify with our fears. Her first flight was to Europe with her husband, a thirteen-hour ordeal. She'd been scared of heights since she was a child and didn't go to the bathroom for thirteen hours on the jumbo jet, convinced if one more person stood up, the whole plane would tip over and crash, killing them all.

Crying, she begged her husband and the stewardess, "I want off this plane! I want to go down!" They pointed out the window and down at the Atlantic Ocean, "Look down there; I don't think you want off!"

Her body tense and her imagination running wild, Melanie looked down below them and thought she saw sharks with their jaws open wide, saying, "Come on down!" Her fears intensified. She got little empathy from her husband. Irritated with her anxiety, he kept reminding her that it was ridiculous to be afraid.

The whole month of travel in Europe was tainted by her dread of getting back on that plane. And this was supposed to be a romantic trip. The return jet was not only much smaller but more turbulent and shaky. The plane was icy cold, adding to her already shivering condition. The hours seemed to go on forever, but finally they landed in Chicago where she immediately hit the runway and started kissing the earth. Two years later Melanie reluctantly agreed to go on a church trip to Israel and Greece, and she endured her traveling companions making fun of her fear of flying the whole trip. *That's it,* she thought. *I've had it with flying; I'm staying on the ground.*

But God, who hates to see us shackled by fear, had other plans. If we have set our hearts on seeking God and knowing him in a deeper way, he usually arranges a way—not for us to escape but to face our fears with his grace. She was offered a flying opportunity she couldn't turn down.

> **I was once on a mission plane. That is always such a wonderful experience! In a large plane you forget that you are up high in the air but in a small plane you see the ground beneath you, the sky around you, and you feel really dependent on the Lord's protection.**
>
> *Corrie ten Boom*

At that time she was the cardiac care nursing supervisor of a large regional hospital. A famous minister came to preach in Oklahoma City, where he suffered a major heart attack. Critically ill, he lay in her cardiac care unit for several days. Finally the family decided to have him flown back to Memphis on an Intensive Air Care Flight and insisted the only nurse they wanted to accompany him was Melanie.

It didn't help that every time she walked into this man's hospital room, the elderly pastor was praying that the plane would crash so he'd be with his wife who had died several years before. This was a man with a reputation for always having his prayers answered.

Although Melanie came up with numerous excuses, the man's family, the doctor, and her own pastor (who was hosting the minister) put pressure on her, insisting no other nurse would do to monitor his multiple medications and IV drips on the intensive care flight. Sick to her stomach with fright at the thought of having to fly to Memphis in a tiny plane, she determined with the Lord that she wasn't going to live that way anymore. She was becoming like people she knew who didn't take trips with their families because of their fear of flying. So Melanie told God she'd go if he would go with her and help her.

That afternoon, still very anxious about the upcoming flight, she left her office and went down to the gift shop. First a ceramic angel holding a little rabbit caught her eye. Next she found a little open book that said, "Faith in God will hold you up when everything else falls." She bought the angel and the paper mache book and put them on her desk, looking at them many times a day. *Faith in God will hold me up when everything else falls,* she thought. The angel reminded her that God sends his angels to take care of things—including intensive care flights and passengers! Her confidence grew a little, enough for her to board the plane.

In flight, she couldn't obsess over her fear because increased air pressure caused the patient's IV drips to double in frequency, which created a huge danger. Handling his medical crises while reminding herself the whole way that "Faith in God will hold me up when everything else falls," she made it to Memphis and then back to Oklahoma City. After that trip on the small ICU jet, Melanie felt she could make it on any airplane. The elderly pastor got back safely to Memphis and lived several more months, while she has enjoyed numerous flights since then.

On High Places

My experience and Melanie's reminded me of Much-Afraid in Hannah Hurnard's wonderful classic *Hind's Feet on High Places,* an extended allegory about how the main character, Much-Afraid, escaped from her Fearing relatives and went with the Shepherd to the High Places where "perfect love casteth out fear."[1]

Much-Afraid had served the Chief Shepherd for several years and longed to please him but found two things hindered her service: physical disfigurement and a lifetime pattern of fear. In fact, she was afflicted not only by her own anxieties but by those passed down through parents and relatives. Much-Afraid was a member of the "Family of Fearings"—relatives she couldn't seem to escape who always tormented and terrified her.

At her request to leave the Valley of Humiliation and the almost certain marriage planned between her and cousin Craven Fear, the Shepherd takes her on a journey to the High Places where perfect love reigns. On the way, he leads her to dangerous precipices and steep mountains.

"I never dreamed you would do anything like this!" Much-Afraid says on one of the steep ledges. "Lead me to an impassable precipice up which nothing can go but deer and goats, when I'm no more like a deer or a goat than is a jellyfish . . . it's too preposterously absurd!"

The Shepherd laughed too. "I love doing preposterous things," he replied. "Why, I don't know anything more exhilarating and delightful than turning weakness into strength, and fear into faith, and that which has been marred into perfection. If there is one thing more than another which I would enjoy doing at this moment it is turning a jellyfish into a mountain goat."[2]

Isn't that just what the Lord does in our lives? Psalm 18:32–33 says: "He fills me with strength and protects me wherever I go. He gives me the surefootedness of a mountain goat upon the crags. He leads me safely along the top of the cliffs" (TLB). Whenever we feel too at ease in our comfort zone, there he goes, bringing us to an impassable cliff or steep place where the only place to go is into his arms . . . turning us from jellyfish to mountain goats who can go to the high places or anywhere else he calls us, because his perfect love casts out our fear. And faith involves letting go and knowing God will catch us.

Who's in Control?

Flying in an airplane, strapped in a seat belt is the ultimate in having no control. And then we see the news: a jet whose rudder fell off, causing it to crash into a Queens, N.Y., neighborhood only a few weeks after the terrorist attacks; or "Human Error

Behind Crash of Major Airlines Plane in Colombia." These reports remind us that we really aren't in control, that life is fragile. Driving our own car or sitting in our living room, we have the illusion of control and safety. As Lynn Parsley, a family counselor, says, "Control is an illusion, but a cherished one."

Even though statistics show that you are eighteen times safer flying in an airplane than you are taking a shower in your own home, still many people struggle with flight anxiety. When two commuter planes crashed a few months apart, even seasoned business travelers who logged thousands of miles of flight time a year got cold feet. Hundreds of them rented cars and drove long distances to avoid flying on commuter planes. Approximately half of passengers drink or take prescription pills to get through a flight. If we're not in control in the air, who is?

Putting Our Lives in His Hands

All our fears—including the fear of flying—represent in some form the fear of death common to all people, writes Elisabeth Elliot in *Keep a Quiet Heart*.

But is it our business to pray into what may happen tomorrow? It is a difficult and painful exercise which saps the strength and uses up the time given us *today*. Once we give ourselves up to God, shall we attempt to get hold of what can never belong to us—*tomorrow*? Our lives are His, our times in His hand, He is Lord over what will happen, never mind what may happen. When we prayed "Thy will be done," did we suppose He did not hear us? He heard indeed, and daily makes our business His and partakes of our lives. If my life is once surrendered, all is well. Let me not grab it back, as though it were in peril in His hand but would be safer in *mine!*[3]

Finding the answer to a fear of death "begins by coming into a relationship with a person; not only believing what the Bible says is true but knowing Jesus personally,"[4] because that opens the door to receiving his promises, especially his promise of eternal life. Surrendering every part of our lives to God, asking him to fill us with his love, his promises, and his hope instead of fear, can literally transform our lives.

Fighting the Good Fight

I've discovered that going to the "High Places" is not only for the challenges we face in this life but also as we look ahead to the life to come. And it's not so much a place as a perspective. I read a reflection by Cynthia Heald recently that helps me get a bigger perspective of all the "flights" and adventures our lifetime journey entails:[5]

"Our son-in-law, Mark, is a fighter pilot," Cynthia says.

While visiting recently, he was able to give us time in the F-15E flight simulator. I actually sat in a cockpit with TV screens in front of me recording my speed, my altitude, and my ability to keep the plane level and on the right path.

I was a couple of minutes into the flight and Mark, who was in the backseat, calmly told me over the earphones, "Oops, you just crashed, let's get you up and going again!"

As I reflected on my experience, I thought how like the Christian life! The evidence around me indicated that I had crashed, but since this was a simulation flight, I was still alive, able to recover and keep flying. And so it is with us—we may be struck down, but we cannot be ultimately destroyed because we have been born again to eternal life and our lives are hidden (concealed, safe, secure) in Christ with God (Col. 3:3).

Realizing that this fleeting, physical life is essentially a simulation frees us from anxiety and gives us inner peace and rest despite our circumstances. "For a righteous man falls seven times, and rises again" (Prov. 24:16 NASB). We may crash, we may be attacked, but we can get up and keep going. This world is not our final destination; we are only flying through!

We still have to climb into the cockpit, taxi to the runway, and take off every day. And in the spiritual realm, we aren't merely passengers. We are fighter pilots, daily fighting the good fight of faith, but the victory is ours and we are "protected by the power of God through faith."

From Fear to Faith

If you experience anxiety when traveling by plane or when you hear the pilot say, "We are flying into a pocket of turbulence in approximately five minutes," keep your seat belt fastened and your tray tables up like they suggest. But also try these ways to help you move from fear to faith:

The knowledge that we are never alone calms the troubled sea of our lives and speaks peace to our souls.

A. W. Tozer

Remember, wherever you are, there God is. I find the best course of action when flying is to put my life in his hands, as I do each day, but especially before a trip—remembering *wherever I am, he is with me.* Psalm 139:7–10 states the truth of this:

> Where can I go from your Spirit?
>   Where can I flee from your presence?
> If I go up to the heavens, you are there;
>   [that's good news if I fly on a small commuter plane!]
>   if I make my bed in the depths, you are there.
> If I rise on the wings of the dawn,
>   if I settle on the far side of the sea,
> [Hopefully, the plane won't land there, but . . .]
> even there your hand will guide me,
>   your right hand will hold me fast.

What good news! No matter where we are, underneath are God's everlasting arms, and we can find peace on the journey.

Focus on God's Word while taking deep, slow breaths. Thinking about God's Word will help you overcome your fear, but speaking the truth builds your faith even more and reminds you that God is your Protector. Verses like "The Lord God is my Strength, my personal bravery, and my invincible army; He makes my feet like hinds' feet and will make me to walk . . . upon my high places" (Hab. 3:19 AMP) remind us that we can trust his grace and protection. Add verses like this one and those at the end of the chapter to your Peace Packet. Memorize verses that bring you comfort and courage so they will be in your mind's "file cabinet," quickly retrievable in fear-producing situations.

Pray specifically! I pray for ministering angels around the plane, the pilot, and all of us passengers when I travel. "For He will give His angels charge concerning you, to guard you in all your ways" is good news when you're in the air! (Ps. 91:11 NASB). And praying specifically for God's angelic protection for your loved ones and friends who fly will also bring peace to your heart and theirs.

When my friend Dorothy's son Richard was in the air force training to fly T-38s, he was thrilled. It was a dream come true, because he had wanted to be a pilot since he was little. His mom, however, was not thrilled. He and the other pilots-in-training would be flying in formation, with the jets only twelve to eighteen inches apart, at extremely high speeds. And she was panicked for him. In Arizona there were blue skies every day, and she knew they'd be up there flying. Worry totally preoccupied her mind.

During this anxious time, a friend visited for lunch and said, "Dorothy, I'm ashamed of you! Why are you worried about Richard? Don't you know God loves him a lot more than you do?" The friend suggested Dorothy pray that day for God to assign an angel to fly on his wing.

Never again did she worry about her youngest son flying. She just prayed each day for an angel to fly on the wing of his plane. In the air force and as a pilot for a major commercial airline for almost thirty years, Richard has had close calls flying in dense fog, snowstorms, and blizzards, but Dorothy has always known the angel on his wing would bring him safely home.

Distract yourself with activity. Staying occupied while in flight is a practical stress reducer. Take a book or magazine, read the in-flight magazine, work on a current project, carry stationery and stamps to catch up on correspondence. If you stay busy, you'll be surprised when the pilot comes on the intercom to say you're almost there.

Remind yourself of some facts:

- You are safer in an airplane than in a car on a highway (or even in your own bed). More people die in their beds than in airplanes.
- Your chance of perishing in an airline crash is 1 in 10 million.
- Your chance of dying from a bee sting is greater than dying in a plane crash.
- You are eighteen times safer flying in a plane than you are taking a shower.

Most importantly, remember the facts from God's Word, like "Safety is of the LORD" (Prov. 21:31 KJV), says Don Gossett.[6] The Bible tells us in Psalm 33:17 a horse, for all its strength, cannot save you. Translated for the twenty-first century: A car, the biggest international airplane, or even our homes with the best security systems aren't what really saves us. Our safety is in the Lord. We are to make wise decisions and take precautions where needed to protect ourselves and our families, but the Lord is our true security, our place of safety.

The Lifeline of God's Word

> Those who live in the shelter
>   of the Most High
>   will find rest in the shadow of the Almighty.
> This I declare of the LORD:
>   He alone is my refuge, my place of safety;
>   he is my God, and I am trusting him.
>
> Psalm 91:1–2 NLT

Lord, you alone are my place of safety. You are my refuge, and I am trusting you. Whether I fly or drive or sit in my home, I will find rest in the shadow of your wings. Because you will shield me and shelter me, I don't have to fear.

> Lord, through all the generations
> you have been our home!
> Before the mountains were created,
> before you made the earth and the world,
> you are God, without beginning or end . . .
> For he orders his angels
> to protect you wherever you go.
> They will hold you with their hands.

Psalm 90:1–2; 91:11–12 NLT

O Lord my God, thank you for commanding your angels to protect me wherever I go. Even before I was conscious of it, you were shielding me and your angels carried me in their arms. Through all generations, whatever happens in this life or the life to come, you are our home, our dwelling place. You are God, without beginning or end!

eleven

Overcoming Childhood Fears

Trust in the dark, trust in the light
trust at night, and trust in the morning.

Hannah Whitall Smith

Amy, a seven-year-old growing up in a small west Texas town, went to sleep one April night as she did most spring evenings, with her jeans, shirt, and tennis shoes on. By the door she had placed her "tornado bag," an old green duffel bag containing her Bible, favorite photographs, a jar of peanut butter with crackers, and her flashlight.

"Don't worry. Your daddy is watching the storm," her mom reminded her when she tucked her in. But that didn't keep Amy from worry and fear. As she lay in bed shivering, arms tight around her teddy bear on that warm spring evening, she kept her ear tuned for the beeping sound on the television that signaled a tornado was coming.

The town lay right in a tornado path, and from March through June, at least three times a week the whole town was alerted because of severe storms that frequently blew through the area. When the alarm sounded, over five hundred people, including Amy's family, would crowd into the community storm cellar, which was the underground level of the elementary school where her father served as principal.

That night Amy was almost asleep in her bed when her father rushed in, grabbed her, and carried her to the car. The TV beeped a high-pitched signal. Amy clutched her little brown poodle puppy and tornado bag to her chest. Just before her dad put her in the backseat, a softball-sized hailstone hit his forearm, splitting it open. Amy watched in horror as blood spurted out from his gash all over her jeans, but it didn't slow her dad down. He had to unlock the school so the townspeople could go in for shelter.

> Each of us has a set of our own "shadow monsters," fears related to past events [that] loom over us at unexpected times. They crowd out present happiness and cast a dark cloud over future success.
>
> *Carol Kent,* Tame Your Fears

Five hundred men, women, children, and crying babies, soon impatient with being crowded together, finally thought the dangerous storm had blown over. People started filing up the stairs. But when Amy's dad looked out the window, telephone poles were flying through the air and masses of debris were whirling. The tornado had turned around, split into three funnels, and was bringing more destruction in its path.

Amy felt absolutely numb that what they had feared for so long was happening. Although houses and businesses all around them were damaged, when they returned to their home later that night, it was still standing. But the physical damage to the town wasn't the worst of the destruction. Following that terrifying night, Amy's fears escalated. She began having nightmares about tornadoes and thunderstorms. She wouldn't go to a friend's house to spend the night unless they had a basement or storm shelter.

As Amy grew into adolescence, her fears didn't dissipate; they spread. She became afraid of being rejected, of failing, of not being perfect. On the outside she acted happy, took part in school activities, and achieved good grades. But on the inside, she was fearful and tormented. This is the way fear operates, spilling over into other areas of a person's life when it is not dealt with. "All children have some sort of fear—either real or imagined—and if they can talk through their fears with compassionate and wise parents, they learn to manage their fears," says Leslie Vernick, licensed clinical social worker and author of *The Truth Principle*. For a child, not talking about their fears, as in Amy's case, or being mocked, rejected, or made fun of, can make the fears larger or more traumatic.

Why couldn't she talk about her fears to anyone? The family she grew up in was *very* private about feelings, and they *especially* didn't talk about their fears. Amy felt she had to be strong and brave for her gentle, somewhat insecure mom. Her dad thought being afraid of storms or anything else was silly, and he told her to buck up or be brave whenever she tried to talk to him about her anxieties. He expected Amy to be logical about things. So her fears remained hidden.

A Deeper Fear

Almost everyone is fearful or anxious at one time or another, especially if we grow up in a place like "tornado alley" where the threat of destruction is a constant in childhood. And most people carry a few childhood fears into adulthood. But for people whose anxiety becomes paralyzing, they can usually trace the onset to some sort of trauma. In Amy's case, that event was not only the massive tornado that struck her town, not only the sexual abuse she experienced at the age of five at the day care center she attended while her mother worked each afternoon but the fact that she was alone in her fears—they were stuffed inside her like all the things tightly stuffed in her "tornado bag."

Growing up in a private family whose members stuffed their feelings, Amy closed everything off even though the abuse incident was extremely traumatic. Her parents didn't know anything about the abuse (or if they did, they didn't do anything that helped Amy through it), so she suffered silently. And while the memories might have faded a little as the years went on, Amy's emotions didn't.

Sometimes the effects of abuse are similar to those suffered by soldiers returning from battle, posttraumatic stress disorder, (PTSD) in which their whole sense of control is destroyed. On the outside, Amy tried hard to maintain a sense of normalcy and control; yet on the inside, her fears escalated. In addition, like many women who are abused, she experienced continual guilt that floated underneath all she did. This guilt, which stems from the misbelief that "If I'd been really good enough or strong enough, I could have kept the abuse from happening," led to low self-esteem that drove her to constant attempts to be thin enough or perfect enough to please the people in her life.

Childhood Fears

Just like keeping a tattered teddy bear from childhood, many times when we don't have the resources to face and resolve childhood conflicts and emotions, we drag them into adult life. For example, as I shared in chapter 9, a child who learns to fear rejection will often experience loneliness and isolation in adulthood. A child caught up in the performance trap by parents who are never satisfied with her achievements will tend to perfectionism and self-condemnation as an adult.

In Amy's case, the childhood fears that reached all the way back to her "tornado bag" nights were alive and well and kept her from moving on with her life. As Robert McGee says, "Fear, in one form or another, usually is why people continue their childhood patterns rather than to 'put childish ways behind them.'"[1]

In college Amy met and married a singer with a Christian band who came into town and swept her off her feet. When the young husband's perfectionism demanded that she look like she walked out of a Hollywood movie, which required working out twice a day and losing weight—when she weighed only one hundred pounds to start—it intensified her fear of failure.

Naïve and inexperienced, she had no concept that abuse could happen in her marriage, but what started out as emotional and verbal progressed in five years of marriage to physical abuse. Afraid of not being thin enough and pretty enough for her husband to love her, she also developed anorexia and bulimia in the process of trying desperately to please him.

> When you stop running and face your fear head-on with faith, you find God. It is His presence and power that move us beyond our fears—past, present, and future.
>
> *Bruce Larson,* Living beyond Our Fears

The abuse cycle fed her fears. When Amy broke emotionally and physically and the marriage failed, she feared God couldn't love her, that her family and the Christian community wouldn't accept her. And although she felt God had some purpose for her, she was afraid she'd never be restored enough to find it.

God Steps In

And then God intervened and began a process of restoration that has continued for several years. After extensive counseling, Bible study, and growth in her Christian life, the healing process progressed as Amy worked through many of her fears and gained some degree of emotional health. She met a wonderful man, and they married and had a daughter.

All seemed well and they were happily married—that is, until her husband had to be away on business trips as a pharmaceutical rep. Suddenly Amy began to experience an intense, irrational jealousy that kept her from trusting her husband. She pictured him with other women on his travels; she worried that he'd leave her although he'd been faithful and loved her dearly. Consumed and in agony, one day she got on her face before God and cried out, "Where is this jealousy coming from? Why can't I get past this?" She begged God to free her.

She had tried everything she knew: listening to tapes, memorizing Scriptures, counseling.

Slowly, the light began to go on. She realized her fear of rejection was underneath the insane jealousy. God seemed to be saying, "Amy, I can deal with whatever comes in your life, like John's traveling or people rejecting you, but you must lay down your fears." He wouldn't make her; it was her choice, an act of her will, to hold on to or give God her fears.

At that point, Amy gave God the "tornado bag" she had held on to all those stormy nights as a child and had carried throughout her life. Filled with the fear of rejection, abuse, and all the other anxieties God brought to her mind, Amy laid the tattered old bag at the feet of Jesus. As she did, a sense swept through her that she could trust God to handle all the uncontrollable events and storms that might blow through her and her family's life.

Did she never feel jealousy or fear again? She did, but every time the fear that her husband was going to be unfaithful came up in her thoughts, she released it to God immediately. She renewed her mind in God's Word and replaced the lies with the truth. Once the fear dissipated, more insights came. The Lord showed her husband a picture of a big root, and the root was rejection. There was a blanket lying on top of it that was her fear, and three prongs held the blanket on securely: unforgiveness, self-hatred, and self-rejection caused by the childhood abuse. With the blanket of fear removed, she was able to deal with the memories of abuse, forgive her abuser, and come into more freedom than she had ever imagined possible. As her trust in God began to increase, faith became the source of her decisions and actions and the foundation of her life instead of anxiety.

The Light Overcomes Darkness

Children's "spiritual windows" and hearts are wide open. Very sensitive, they can be profoundly influenced by both positive and negative spiritual influences. Sometimes even brief contact with a person can make a lifelong impact and produce fear. Taylor had struggled with feeling afraid since she was a very little

131

girl. When she grew up, the fears didn't go away. As an adult, she went through seasons where she would wake up feeling paralyzed and terrified—oftentimes with no apparent cause. This would cause her to get up late, be physically tired and drained, and not spend time with the Lord. Then her whole day would get off to a wrong start and she'd feel like she was running behind.

Taylor and her husband were already seeing marriage counselors twice a month, and she mentioned her struggle with fear to them after a series of bad nights. As they talked that evening, the problem with fear was narrowed down specifically to fear of the demonic. "How strange," Taylor told them. "I never played with Tarot cards or Ouija boards or was involved with anything related to the occult. I even avoided horror movies because they made me more afraid." Her counselors prayed that the source, the place where the fear originally took root, would be revealed.

Suddenly a picture came to Taylor's mind of one of her dad's friends who was at their home quite frequently. When she saw the picture of his face on the movie screen of her mind, it turned very ugly, like a demon. His fingernails turned into sharply pointed claws. She realized that through being around this man, a fear of the demonic had attached itself to her. When she spoke to her father about the fears she had struggled with and the memory of his friend, he said if he had known then what he does now as a Christian, he wouldn't ever have been friends with the man or allowed him into their home. He lived with his common-law wife, abused alcohol, was into sexual perversion, and was a negative influence on her dad's life before her dad met Christ.

The next time they met, Taylor's counselors prayed that this fear of the demonic would be broken over her life. They asked her to confess her sin in believing that the demonic was more powerful than God. John 1:5 came to mind: The light will never be overcome by darkness. Since then, if Taylor does wake up afraid, which is rare, she now knows that the fear is not from God and that she doesn't have to put up with it. She refuses the fear and stands against the enemy by proclaiming, "In the name of Jesus, Satan, I command you to leave. I give no place to you.

I resist your spirit of fear for I belong to the Lord Jesus Christ, and greater is he that is within me than you who are in the world." She reminds herself of John 1 and that Jesus overcame her fear for her—his light will never be overcome by darkness!

My Bagful of Childhood Fears

As I have shared in previous chapters, I too had a whole bagful of childhood fears. Some of these I used to say I received "in utero" from my precious, fearful mother, who though wonderful and loving, was afraid of many things—from thunderstorms to flying in an airplane, to accidents, swimming, poverty, to a dreaded fear of anything happening to one of her six kids—to name a few.

Perhaps Mom's fears stemmed from her big brother dying of blood poisoning in childhood after his foot was run over by a milk truck, and her mother, then pregnant with her, being traumatized by the loss. Maybe it was seeing her other brother fall off their porch backward and have a grand mal epileptic seizure, a problem that would afflict him his whole life. Or maybe it was living through desperate times during the Great Depression and being left with her unemployed, alcoholic father and brothers without proper provision for her needs while her mother often traveled with her professional dancing twin sisters.

Whatever the causes, Mom's fears were transferred to us by words we heard often, like: *Don't lean your head on the seat at the movie theater; you might get ringworm . . . Don't go to bed with a wet head; you'll get sick with a cold.* Fear limited our life in certain other ways. Mom didn't drive, and she almost never flew in an airplane.

While there often are generational fears that plagued our ancestors and thus have easy access into our lives (which is a whole subject I do not have the expertise or space to address here), more likely I grew fearful because as Barbara Sullivan says in *The Control Trap,* "when parents are fearful themselves, they communicate fear to their children . . . soon the child feels that the world is a fearful, threatening place."[2] And then I developed my own set of fears from experiences in early life like the car trauma in New Mexico I related earlier, and Papa's, Grandfather's, and my aunt's tragic deaths so close together as well as a close friend's my age two years later. These events all combined to produce my fear of loss and death.

What brought me out of the grip of childhood fears? It was a *process,* not an overnight event. In a sense, my fears drove me to the end of myself and into the arms of God. But once I truly turned my life over to him and began to walk in a day-by-day relationship with Christ when I was twenty-nine years old, I began to experience his faithfulness and realized that though I had felt abandoned by my father, who had died, and later a stepfather who couldn't be depended on, Jesus would never leave me or forsake me. Though I had a fear of not measuring up that stemmed from my father's very high expectations of us (As were expected, not celebrated), I began to experience that the Lord wasn't demanding a performance or always expecting me to work harder to get his approval. In fact, he loved and accepted me and wanted me to come and give him my burdens and rest in his arms just the way I was, even when I was tired or not measuring up.

Along the way, God's Word renewed my mind and thoughts, and I realized that when I was afraid, I could trust in his Word and his character (Psalm 56); that he is my rock and my refuge; that nothing is impossible to him; that nothing can separate me from his love (Rom. 8:39). These and many other Scriptures I share in this book gave me a new perspective on life, new courage and faith in God, and a sense of adventure instead of anxiety.

Awareness dawned and my heart opened up so that when the circumstances and problems of life pressed in and fears resurfaced, I asked for help and root causes were brought into the light. Healing came through the ministry of the Holy Spirit in a few short-term sessions with a Christian counselor from time to time when I was in a stressful season. Later, more healing came through our church, where being in a small support group gave me insight on my family of origin and helped me face some deeper emotional issues like my fear of anger and my sense of insecurity. And the light and healing continued as God gave people spiritual discernment and insight into my life and they prayed with me (people such as Peter Marshall; Diana, a Christian psychologist; and women at our church who direct the Shelter and Boundaries groups).

Although childhood fears impacted my adult life, I have experienced God's healing and deliverance, and I know nothing is too difficult for him. He wants us to give him our fears, both from childhood and those we are presently struggling with. He wants us to be open to allow his Spirit to search our hearts and memories for the roots of those fears. Moreover, he wants *you* to be free just as he did Amy, Taylor, and me—free to live and move and have your being in Christ (Acts 17:28) without being in bondage to old fears or anxieties. He died that we might live without fear and live life to the full. For she whom the Son has set free is free indeed!

> **The way to take the fear out of living is to put faith in the Lord.**
>
> *Croft M. Pentz*

From Fear to Faith

Childhood fears, as we have seen in this chapter, can subtly but powerfully impact your adult life. But no matter how far back they go, your childhood fears can be overcome.

You may have received a legacy of fear, but you can overcome those fears and live in faith, boldly and confidently following the Lord and not filled with dread, anxiety, or worry. Here are some ways to start:

Open the doors of your heart to God's healing power. God can help you deal with any problem and gain healing from whatever abuse or trauma produced the childhood fears you've carried with you into adult life, but it is your part to lay your fears at his feet. First it takes opening your heart to him, like David in the Psalms asked: "Search me, O God, and know my heart; test me and know my anxious thoughts. See if there is any offensive [hurtful] way in me, and lead me in the way everlasting" (Ps. 139:23–24). Pray that God will show you what is behind the fears you have struggled with. Maybe it's a feeling of dread that won't go away or a persistent sense of anxiety.

When these surface, ask: *Where did this fear take root? Where did it begin?*

Sometimes we are too close to the forest to see the trees, too close to the problems in our own lives to have much insight about them, especially if our fears have been hiding behind denial, workaholism, perfectionism, or other self-protective strategies. A small support group is vital if there has been any abuse, or even if you just have deeply rooted issues you're trying to work through. Recovery is longer and lonelier when we try to do it alone. Participating in groups helps you to realize that you are not alone. As you listen to others struggle with the same lies that you have told yourself, i.e., "I'm no good; it was all my fault" or "I will always have these problems; there's no hope for me" and as you empathize with their pain, you can more easily identify your own internal lies and begin to replace them with God's truth.

If you find yourself struggling with past abuse or other traumas that are impacting your present life, look for a trusted counselor who can help you face your past and see beyond the present to where the pattern of fear began in your life. Ask for prayer and be open to God's Spirit and his work in your life. As Carol Kent says in her book *Tame Your Fears,* "Every day I have a choice. Will I allow fear to overcome me, or will I take action, even though the results are not guaranteed, and look with faith into the face of my Savior?"[3]

Once you've identified them, give your fears to God. Write down the things you are afraid of and release them to him. We tend to take our fears everywhere *except* to God. We might tell our best friend, the crisis hot line, our sister across the country. It's great to have friends when you are stressed or afraid (oh, how we need our friends), but God is the One who can do something about our fear and the problem that's behind it or causing it. "God can and will provide whatever we need to get beyond our painful emotions, but only if we are willing to be honest about them," says Robert McGee.[4] What specific fears do you need to be honest about, let go of, and give to God?

Try giving your fears and worries to God with some concrete gesture. You could put your list in a small box or bag and keep it as a reminder that on this date you put a stake down and laid down your fears. Just getting your fears on paper brings them into the light and they lose some of their power over you. One prayer group has a "God Box." Each week as they pray about their lives and problems, they put slips of paper with the things they have given to the Lord in the "God Box." This reminds them that these issues are *his* and that they have given their problems and fears to God.

If anxiety persists, seek medical help. Remember that some anxiety, panic, and fearfulness are components of clinical depression and biochemical imbalances in the brain and can't be alleviated by counseling, prayer, or Scripture reading alone. In some cases anxiety and panic have a biochemical root (perhaps coexisting with other emotional and spiritual roots) and can be greatly relieved by medication and therapy.

As Dr. Paul Meier says, "You can do more to stop your anxieties than you ever thought. However, when medication is needed—*it's needed!* If our bodies aren't producing the right chemicals in proper balance, we need to add medicines to restore order. Taking medical preparations is *not* a defeat of your faith or will power." If there's a true chemical imbalance, the right medication prescribed in the proper manner and time can be a Godsend, Meier says.[5] Get a complete physical exam from your family doctor. Seek help with a licensed psychologist or psychiatrist in addition to continuing your own devotional life, prayer, and Bible study. Apply the suggestions in this book. Also, consider a weekly support group or Bible study using the questions for reflection and discussion in the third part of this book as a format. Small groups are particularly effective for those with anxiety. We often think we are the only ones who are afraid, so there is tremendous support and healing in dealing with these issues in a group setting.

The Lifeline of God's Word

> God has not given us a spirit of fear and timidity, but of power, love, and self-discipline [a sound mind].

> 2 Timothy 1:7 NLT

Lord, thank you that you haven't appointed me to live fearfully. You haven't given me a spirit of fear. On the contrary, through the death and resurrection of your Son, Jesus Christ, and by sending the Spirit to live in our hearts by faith, you have given me a spirit of power, of love, and a sound mind. *Help me to enter into what you have already provided! Open my heart to receive your healing.* Here are the fears I am struggling with today: _____
I ask you to give me insight into their origin and source, and to deliver me by your mighty power so I can freely and abundantly live according to the purposes you have for my life.

> The LORD your God is with you,
>   he is mighty to save.
> He will take great delight in you,
>   he will quiet you with his love,
>   he will rejoice over you with singing.

Zephaniah 3:17

> From the ends of the earth I call to you,
>   I call as my heart grows faint;
>   lead me to the rock that is higher than I.
> For you have been my refuge,
>   a strong tower against the foe.

Psalm 61:2–3

Lord, thank you that you are with me and you are mighty to save! Thank you that you take great delight in me and will quiet me with your love as you rejoice over me with singing. Help me to get a glimpse of this amazing truth, Lord. When my heart grows faint, lead me to the Rock Who is higher than I. Lead me by your Spirit into an intimate relationship with you, for you have been my refuge. You are my shelter and protection. And you are a strong tower against any foes.

twelve

Overcoming a Fear of Failure

Part of the Christian style of life involves a spontaneity in which we lose our fear of failure and move out in the light of the guidance that we have.

Keith Miller, *The Edge of Adventure*

Have you ever been afraid to fail? Whether it's anxiety before a big exam or job interview, a fear of public speaking or trying to paint a picture, we've all experienced the nervousness, shaky hands, dry mouth, and anxious thoughts that accompany a fear of failure. Sometimes we're afraid to say a prayer aloud in a group, teach a Bible study, or even ask a question in a Sunday school class. Or we bail out of a project at work because we feel inadequate or make excuses when asked to perform in the Christmas play at church.

I remember a woman I met while I was volunteering at a children's hospital. She was serving as librarian and truly loved books. In fact, she informed me, she was working on a master's degree in creative writing. "I have a children's book I've written that I wish I could get published," she said one day when she found out I was a writer.

"Did you write a proposal and send it out?" I asked.

"No, I was afraid it would be rejected. I couldn't stand failing like that," she answered sadly.

This woman had a burning interest in writing, had taken courses for five years, gotten a master's degree in creative writing, and even written articles in addition to the children's book. Yet her fears kept her from taking the next step—sending her work off to prospective publishers.

> He only fails who never attempts.
>
> *Anonymous*

It reminds me of the cartoon in "The Family Circus" cartoon strip by Bill Keane in which two kids are peering inside a grand piano. The little girl instructs the small boy, "There are millions of songs in there, but you hafta punch the right keys to get them out." God gives us inspiration—great ideas, gifts and talents, words to write and songs to play—but we have to apply the perspiration and punch those keys, even risking rejection and failure along the way.

Every one of us is gifted. God created each of us with a combination of gifts, talents, and strengths—inner abilities that can be displayed in a performance or used in a business, ministry, or creative situation. Perhaps you are the one who thinks of a creative solution to any problem. Maybe you can organize a big event or teach a Bible study. Music may be your gift, or encouragement or compassionate serving. Whatever the gift, the Lord wants us to pick that strength or combination of strengths and pursue it with the same abandon and enthusiasm as Eric Liddell, the Scottish missionary to China and Olympic runner, did.

In a great scene in *Chariots of Fire,* the movie about Liddell's path to the Olympic gold medal, Eric stands on a green Scottish hillside while his sister Jenny scolds him for not being at the mission enough because of his daily running practice, preparing for the Olympic trials. "How could you let me down? How could you let God down?" she complains, attempting to stir up his guilt so he'll come with her to the mission instead of practicing.

"But God made me fast," he tells his sister. "And when I run, I feel his pleasure." Because Eric Liddell pursued the gift God gave him, a whole country was impacted by his message and generations after that were inspired by his faith; and he gave the rest of his life to mission work back in China.

Similarly, when we use the gifts and talents God gives us—whether they are running, composing music, writing, teaching, coordinating events, or directing a business—we feel God's smile; we sense his pleasure. And we are filled with pure joy. Also, when we are using the gifts God gave us, whether they are spiritual, mental, or creative gifts, we operate in a maximum of effectiveness and a minimum of weariness because we are doing what he made us to do.

I believe that a big part of our purpose on earth is connected to these particular gifts and talents God has entrusted to us. But often, because of fear of failure, we fail to use them. Remember the parable of the talents? A man gave five thousand coins to one servant, two thousand to the second, and one thousand to the third. Then he left the country. When he came back and checked on how his servants had done, he praised and rewarded the first, who had doubled his money. The second said, "Master, I made a 50 percent profit on your money," and he was also rewarded.

But the next servant said, "Master, here's your money safe and sound. I kept it hidden in the cellar. To tell you the truth, I was a little afraid. I know you have high standards and hate sloppiness, and don't suffer fools gladly."

"You're right," the Master said. "But why didn't you at least invest the money in securities so I would have gotten a little interest on it?" So he took the money from him and gave it to the productive servant who doubled his talent.

They said, "But Master, he already has double."

He said, "That's what I mean: Risk your life and get more than you ever dreamed of. Play it safe and end up holding the bag" (Luke 19:11–27 MESSAGE).

Clammy Hands

I can identify with those servants, especially the one who hid his talent because of fear. There were several things I had said I wouldn't do because I was afraid, and public speaking was at the top of the list. I was too petrified to speak in front of any group. My hands got clammy, my mouth got dry, and I feared people's disapproval.

But the Lord has creative ways of helping us face our fears and pursue what he has planned for us. He continued to work on my fears, peeling them back like an onion, layer by layer. And each adversity I faced became a tool God used to bring me into more freedom and growth instead of more anxiety.

One of these times was when my fifty-nine-year-old mom was diagnosed with cancer and told she had one to six months to live. She set about getting the treatment she could, but she also set about to do the practical things to get her life in order. Mom had always been a very organized planner, so she wrote our names under the furniture she wanted us to have and divided her jewelry "so we wouldn't squabble," she said. She was torn, wanting to be well and to keep having her grandkids out to the ranch and to do her favorite things like gardening and going to church. It was agonizingly hard to let us go, but she said to me one night, "I'll get to see Jesus face to face. After praying to him all these years about all of you, now I can talk to him about you up close."

She then asked me to write down the songs and plans for her "Glorious Homecoming" service, as she called it. "Great Is Thy Faithfulness," "Special Delivery," and the Scriptures she wanted read.

"Now don't forget that little chorus from Isaiah 61." I'd sung it to her daily in trying moments . . . when she had radiation or other treatment and was in pain, she would say, "Sing 'Beauty for Ashes' for me." Somehow that Scripture song always seemed to lift her spirits.

God had put that chorus in my mind when I was coming back to Dallas from Oklahoma City after hearing her diagnosis. *Lord,*

I want to be there for Mama. I want to be strong and be there for her. She has always been there for me. Where will I get the strength? That's when the song began to run through my mind, "He gives me beauty for ashes, the oil of joy for mourning, the garment of praise for the spirit of heaviness that we might be trees of righteousness, the planting of the Lord, that he might be glorified."

"Be sure it's sung at my service," Mama said, "and if no one in the choir can sing it, you sing it for me. It's very important to me. Will you promise?"

> **Oh, but man's reach should exceed his grasp or what's a heaven for?**
>
> *Robert Browning*

You don't argue with your mom when she's planning her funeral! Writing it down on the list, I felt sure the soloist, choir, or music director at her church would sing it. But when Mom died two weeks later, I gave the directions to the pastor. A few hours later he came by and said, "Everything's planned just as your mother wanted it, but no one in the choir has ever heard of that song."

"But it just goes like this, 'He gave me beauty for ashes, the oil of joy for mourning,'" I sang. "Just like in the verses in the Bible. Surely someone can sing that simple melody."

"No one wants to do it on short notice," he replied. "It's a good thing you know it because if it's sung, *you'll* have to do it."

The next morning I woke up heavyhearted and exhausted from nights at the hospital. There was a hole in my heart and I missed Mama already. I was neither a professional singer nor in any shape to sing at the funeral, and I knew it. But I didn't want to break my promise to her, either. That morning in my quiet time, I said, "Lord, I can't do this. But I don't want to let Mama down."

He clearly directed me to the reading that morning, Romans 12:1: "Present your bodies a living and holy sacrifice, acceptable to God, which is your spiritual service of worship" (NASB). God seemed to be saying, "Just present yourself to me as a vessel and I'll do the rest."

Later that day at Mama's service, I stood up (with my husband and three kids joining in), banked by sprays of red roses and white carnations, and sang a cappella the little chorus from Isaiah 61.

I didn't feel like an oak of righteousness, but God gave me the strength just at the moment I needed it to sing the song I'd promised Mama. What I didn't realize at the time was how God would use that verse and the truth that I learned.

I'd been keeping journals and writing poems about my children for several years. The desire to write was growing, yet all my pieces of writing were stuck in file drawers. Right after my mother died, I was reminded how brief life is and felt an urgency that I needed to get on with learning the craft of writing. I took a six-week freelance writers' course to learn some basics, continued my journaling, and wrote a few articles and submitted a few of my poems, most of which were rejected.

The next year I taught in high school and was struck by how unmotivated and troubled the teenagers were and how their academic skills had fallen since the last time I'd been in the classroom, only a few years before. And this was a private Christian school! Parents seemed frustrated and puzzled about what to do about their children's poor performance.

While grading at my desk one afternoon during the spring semester, I began to pray for and weep over my students. Suddenly, the outline for a book for parents came to me with the title clearly in my mind: *HOME-LIFE: The Key to Your Child's Success at School.* Even the name of each chapter occurred to me. I was so excited about the idea that when the semester ended, I "retired" from teaching, got a word processor with a little money left behind by Mama, and started to "Just do it!" With my book proposal all typed and a sample chapter under my arm, I went to a writers' conference in Minnesota that summer to learn how to write a nonfiction book.

Step by Step

It was a step-by-step process. God only showed me a glimpse, one step to take at a time. I would take it, and he would show me one more step and open a door. But he always provided the light to take that next step.

About two-thirds of the way through the writing of my book, the publisher interested in the project dropped it. In the meantime I sent one chapter to a major secular women's magazine and a major Christian magazine and had them both accept it as a feature article. Months later, I met a publisher over lunch at a writers' conference and was offered a contract within a week. I finished the book while we were packing to move to Maine. Then nine months later in September of 1988, the book was released and my articles came out—all in the same week. This not only led to having to fly to New York City to be on *NBC Radio News* and other radio programs but being asked to speak to parents' and teachers' groups.

At that point, God and I had a little chat. "Lord! I didn't sign up to speak. I just said I would do this one book for parents and write some articles to help equip them to support their children's learning."

The Lord knew all the time I'd be "Much-Afraid," like the character in Hannah Hurnard's book *Hind's Feet on High Places,* if he had shown me the whole blueprint right from the start. So he led me one step at a time. "Lord, help!" I cried, my stomach in knots just thinking about speaking to the group that invited me.

"Remember your mother's service? What did I show you to do?" his Spirit seemed to say. "Like in Romans 12:1, just offer yourself to me as a living sacrifice and I'll do the rest."

When I got up to address the parents' group of Yarmouth Intermediate School that first night, my hands were a little shaky and my mouth was dry. But as I began to talk, peace filled me and I began to feel a crazy sense of joy sharing with the group of eager parents. I've been speaking ever since for fifteen years, and I usually experience that same irrepressible joy I felt that night in Yarmouth, Maine. God "is able to do exceedingly abundantly above all that we ask or think, according to the power at work within us" (Eph. 3:20 NKJV).

Not that the journey hasn't had twists, turns, obstacles, and difficulties, like flying into a blizzard into the mountains of

Wyoming to speak to all the parents in the town. My luggage was lost and I had nothing to wear except the jeans I had on! Or like speaking seventeen times in ten days in Chiang Mai, Thailand, while trying to recover from a terrible intestinal bacteria. But through it all, God has continued to refine, prepare, and help me face and overcome more of my fears.

You Are Not Alone

If you have ever been afraid of addressing an audience, whether it be your colleagues at work or a group at church, you are not alone. Research shows that the fear of public speaking is one of the top fears people struggle with.[1] The fear of talking before an audience is greater than the fear of death, snakes, insects, and accidents. College surveys indicate that 80 to 90 percent of all students taking speech courses struggle with stage fright at the beginning of the course. Dale Carnegie stated that the statistics were even higher for adults: 100 percent of those taking his "How to Succeed" courses throughout the years were afraid of speaking in front of an audience.[2]

> The adventurous life is not one exempt from fear, but on the contrary one that is lived in full knowledge of fears of all kinds, one in which we go forward in spite of our fears.
>
> *Paul Tournier*

But there are other fears that hold us back from using the potential God has given us. Sharon's fear began when she stepped outside her door as a young woman into a critical world that would judge her based on what she knew and how she behaved.[3] She constantly worried about what others thought of her. As she grew, her fears started robbing her of golden opportunities. She turned down invitations to the high school prom because she didn't think she was a good dancer and was afraid of being laughed at. In college, fear of failure caused her to blow a lucrative newspaper internship. She failed to show up for the job. At age thirty, her fears developed into full-scale panic attacks with tightness in her throat, heart palpitations, extreme terror, and mental anguish. Everything she used to do with ease became a major task.

Sharon sought help from a holistic doctor who insisted the solution to her problem was "manipulating the negative energy" in her body through massage. That helped her be relaxed temporarily, but the fears returned when she got home. Going to a hypnotist didn't reveal why she was having panic attacks or cure them. Then she turned to her medical doctor for help, and he prescribed sedatives. After spending several hundred dollars searching for a cure and coming up empty, she finally turned to God and began attending church for the first time in years. The songs and Scriptures calmed her nerves so much she began carrying a Bible with her all the time. Day by day, God would lead her to specific Scriptures. Six months later, her panic attacks were gone.

With renewed confidence, Sharon began to work as a public relations specialist and to write professionally. Eventually she pursued a more challenging job: director of public relations at a university's business school. Sometimes the magnitude of her new responsibilities was overwhelming and the familiar fear that had gripped her stomach would return. But she managed to hold on to her job. Every time she planned to jump ship, someone encouraged her to stay. At the roughest points, she would receive a glowing evaluation or hear an inspiring message on Christian radio. In the midst of her fear, the Lord gave her small but meaningful victories.

Sharon began to submit some of her writing and won several competitions. That encouraged her to write a novel, and the book became an overnight success. Months before, she would have panicked over the attention and the radio and television interviews she had to do. But for the first time in her life, she was actually relaxed in front of a TV camera. That was the moment she realized God had healed her. From time to time, she still gets a little anxious when facing the public or about her career. But now she knows that God will carry her through whatever she has to do. He is bigger than her fears. And the more she seeks and trusts him, the more he steers her toward the unique purpose he created her for. God created her to write, to be director of publications at a university, to do all the things she is doing, and neither fear nor anxiety could stop his divine plan.

Fearing Failure

Sometimes a fear of failure—that "unconscious knot that forms in the pit of our stomach"—results from living in a perfectionistic home, shame or a poor self-image, comparison to others, lack of affirmation by parents, or a conditional love based only on achievement. It can happen anywhere and at any age. You have an important decision to make but are afraid you'll make a choice that brings failure. You have a great idea to share but don't know how it will be received.[4]

You may think that only people who suppose themselves without talent are scared to step out and try something new. But even when a person is gifted and prepared to do a project, the fear of failure can paralyze her efforts.

Katherine, an artist, heard a message several years ago on what Jesus really suffered at crucifixion. She was struck by what his actual experience at the cross must have been. It also started her thinking about all the paintings she'd seen of the crucifixion. She searched for weeks in art museums and books to find an image that depicted what she had learned.

> That we are alive today is proof positive that God has something for us to do today.
>
> *Vachel Lindsay*

"I had studied art all my life, and the more I looked, the more I realized there was nothing painted of the crucifixion like what I heard in the message," Katherine says. She couldn't get free of those thoughts and kept asking God, "Lord, why hasn't this ever been painted? You've had such spiritual people, such gifted people."

God seemed to answer her, "It's for you to do."

Katherine was daunted as she contemplated the enormity of such a painting. But she dove into the research and preparation process. For the next four months, she studied Scriptures, paintings, and photos and compiled information from the library and the art museum reading room. It was a wonderful time, blessed with a sense of closeness with God.

But as her research was completed and it was time to start the painting, she started looking at her own inability and inadequacy to paint such a work. *How could I even think I could accomplish such a project? Who do I think I am, Michelangelo?* Her fear of failure paralyzed her day after day, and she couldn't pick up a brush to start. At the same time, it seemed like God stopped talking to her and she felt distant from him.

After the richness of what she had shared with God, the two-month silence that followed was frightening. She started scrambling, searching in her quiet times in the Bible, taking more detailed notes in church, trying to figure out what was wrong. One day she felt so alone she prayed from Psalm 51, "Take not Your Holy Spirit from me" (v. 11 AMP).

She was led to the story of the fig tree that Jesus told in Luke 13:

> "A man had a fig tree growing in his vineyard. One day he went out to pick some figs, but he didn't find any. So he said to the gardener, 'For three years I have come looking for figs on this tree, and I haven't found any yet. Chop it down! Why should it take up space?'
>
> "The gardener answered, 'Master, leave it for another year. I'll dig around it and put some manure on it to make it grow. Maybe it will have figs on it next year. If it doesn't, you can have it cut down.'"

PROMISE

Meditating on that passage, Katherine felt like God was saying, "*You* are the fig tree."

She realized he had nurtured her, given her the idea, planted her in a good place, offered every opportunity to do the research and accomplish this work. But she was barren. Suddenly she knew if she didn't put her hand to the work, the talent would wither.

If that wasn't enough nudging, the Lord gave her the picture of how her being stymied by fear was like the Israelites going into Canaan. The whole camp was paralyzed with fear because of a report about the giants in the land, even though God had promised victory. They were looking at their inability to fight the giants and take the land. The Holy Spirit showed her that in the spirit the painting was accomplished—it was her "Promised Land," but she was so paralyzed with fear that she had avoided doing her part—to pick up the brush and paint!

"Okay, Lord, how do I begin?" she finally said.

What she heard made sense to her as an artist: "Line upon line; just make a start and I'll be with you." God's grace pulled Katherine out of a tailspin. For the next six months she painted and completed the work: a large, eight-by-seven-foot, life-sized painting titled *Tetelestar,* which means "paid in full." It hangs in Katherine's studio, and droves of people from various cities and states have come to see it. Although Katherine still considers it not quite complete in the sense of not being ready to make prints of, she is grateful for the opportunity to be a vessel, to get to hold the brush and paint it.

From Fear to Faith

Whether you are afraid of trying something new you always wanted to tackle like art lessons, accepting a challenging new position you're offered at work, writing a book, or entering a marathon, don't let the fear of failure derail you. Whatever your gift is, remember, all gifts were inspired by the same Spirit (1 Cor. 12:11): leading and motivating people, creative ability, people skills, gifts of teaching, mercy, and encouragement, musical talent, organization and administration, nurturing children. Here are some ways to start taking small steps toward using the talents God has given you and living in freedom and faith:

List some of your personal strengths. Creative or inner abilities, skills you have learned, innate intelligence for certain tasks, spiritual gifts, etc. Then pick one that you really want to pursue and develop.

List activities you fear and usually avoid. Break one of these down into several smaller steps and list them. Then start doing the steps you have listed and meet the challenge, little by little.

Share your dream or goal with someone. Sharing your idea or goal with a trusted friend helps bring it out of fantasy and into reality. Discuss how you are going to begin pursuing your passion.

Seek out people who are positive and believe in you. If there is just one person who believes in you and supports you, it can make all the difference. We all need a support system and need to be around people who build up instead of criticize and tear down, especially when we are embarking on a new direction.

Build your faith in God to battle your fear of failure. Just as Sharon experienced, as her faith in the Lord grew larger, her fear of failure grew smaller. Her anxieties didn't paralyze her or block her potential because she knew she could depend on God and he was her strength. He has plans for your life as well, "plans to prosper you and not to harm you, plans to give you hope and a future," the Lord says in Jeremiah 29:11–13. "Then you will call upon me and come and pray to me, and I will listen to you. You will seek me and find me when you seek me with all your heart." Seek God with your whole heart and watch as he guides you in purposes greater than you could ask or think or imagine.

Don't let a little "anticipatory anxiety" hold you back. Whatever talent you possess, when you find it, just do it. It helps to prepare and do your homework. But avoid letting that nervousness or anticipatory anxiety trap you into giving up. Like marathon runners who learn to move through the pain and keep running, learn to move through your jitters. A little bit of stage fright can have a positive effect, propelling you by raising your respiration and speeding up your heart. Even seasoned speakers and performers experience it. The result: you can think faster, talk more flu-

your lap. For with the measure you use, it will be measured to you.

Luke 6:38

The young lions do lack and suffer hunger;
But they who seek the LORD shall not be in want of any
  good thing.

Psalm 34:10 NASB

Write each verse on a 3x5 card and carry the cards with you. If you start worrying, get them out and review them. As you meditate on God's promises daily, say the verse in your own words, telling God you are depending on him. Then continue to add promises from your own Bible reading that build your confidence in God and his ability to provide.

Share the burdens. Even those who have wealth aren't always exempt from fears about finances. Nationally known financial consultant Ron Blue said recently that prosperity leads to fear of loss, and fear of loss leads to loss of faith. Whatever your anxieties or concerns are about finances, give them to God one by one and be specific about your needs. Talk and pray about these heavy burdens with a friend. If anxious thoughts about your financial situation resurface, which they often do, give them back to God right then. Release them as many times as necessary until your mind is free from fretting about them.

Don't be like the little boy who took his broken bicycle to the repair shop to be fixed. The repairman assured him it would be as good as new and told him to leave his bike in the repair room. The repairman promised to call when he was finished fixing it. But after being home for a day or two, the boy began to worry about his bike: *Can the repairman really fix the problem? Is he going to call me or lose my bike? Why isn't it ready yet?* Before he knew it, the little boy raced down to the shop and reclaimed his bicycle—still broken.

You and I are much like that little boy. We may give our financial problem to God, but moments or hours later, we take it back—and start handling it ourselves. If you find you've reclaimed your

The silver-haired pastor began to read Psalm 139 to Mom: "O LORD, you have searched me and you know me. You know when I sit and when I rise; you perceive my thoughts from afar."

Then he stopped at verse 16: "All the days ordained for me were written in your book before one of them came to be."

Suddenly, as Mama heard those verses read aloud, the truth of God's Word moved from her head deep into her heart. She didn't have to worry about how many days she had left, because they were already written in his book. In fact, those words set Mom free to check herself out of the hospital the next morning, be wheeled in a wheelchair to a jet, and have the most glorious flight of her life into a brilliant purple glow of the Texas sunset to a great homecoming in the DFW terminal. It gave her the chance to hold her new grandson, baby Zachary, in her arms and hug her beloved six children, twenty-two grandchildren, and friends . . . and also to celebrate every day she had left on this earth as a gift from the God who had planned and ordained each one of the days throughout her whole life.

Through seeing Mom freed from her fear of flying and her anxiety about "how many days," the truth of Psalm 139 also deepened in my own life. I came to rest in a sense of God's amazing sovereignty—whether on the ground or in the air, whether flying on a jumbo jet across the country after 9-11 to a speaking engagement or on a little prop plane into the snow-covered mountains of Wyoming to do a parent event.

As I finished my story, Maria asked, "Where were those verses you were talking about?" I got out my Bible and read them to her. And a short time later, right before the plane landed, I felt nudged to ask her, "Could I pray for you concerning your fear?"

"Please do," she responded. As I finished my prayer, I thought how kind of God that he put me right next to someone who suffered a fear I had struggled with. And how wise that he had put me in the sky time after time over the years as I flew to speaking engagements, often enough to face my fears and to learn to enjoy flying. All those flying opportunities gave me a chance to become "desensitized" as the experts call it, because when we

I resist your spirit of fear for I belong to the Lord Jesus Christ, and greater is he that is within me than you who are in the world." She reminds herself of John 1 and that Jesus overcame her fear for her—his light will never be overcome by darkness!

My Bagful of Childhood Fears

As I have shared in previous chapters, I too had a whole bagful of childhood fears. Some of these I used to say I received "in utero" from my precious, fearful mother, who though wonderful and loving, was afraid of many things—from thunderstorms to flying in an airplane, to accidents, swimming, poverty, to a dreaded fear of anything happening to one of her six kids—to name a few.

Perhaps Mom's fears stemmed from her big brother dying of blood poisoning in childhood after his foot was run over by a milk truck, and her mother, then pregnant with her, being traumatized by the loss. Maybe it was seeing her other brother fall off their porch backward and have a grand mal epileptic seizure, a problem that would afflict him his whole life. Or maybe it was living through desperate times during the Great Depression and being left with her unemployed, alcoholic father and brothers without proper provision for her needs while her mother often traveled with her professional dancing twin sisters.

Whatever the causes, Mom's fears were transferred to us by words we heard often, like: *Don't lean your head on the seat at the movie theater; you might get ringworm . . . Don't go to bed with a wet head; you'll get sick with a cold.* Fear limited our life in certain other ways. Mom didn't drive, and she almost never flew in an airplane.

While there often are generational fears that plagued our ancestors and thus have easy access into our lives (which is a whole subject I do not have the expertise or space to address here), more likely I grew fearful because as Barbara Sullivan says in *The Control Trap,* "when parents are fearful themselves, they communicate fear to their children . . . soon the child feels that the world is a fearful, threatening place."[2] And then I developed my own set of fears from experiences in early life like the car trauma in New Mexico I related earlier, and Papa's, Grandfather's, and my

ently and with greater inspiration.[5] And the more you speak, the more you'll enjoy it.

Along the way, in whatever you do as you use your gifts and talents, do as Colossians 3:23 says, "Work hard and cheerfully at whatever you do, as though you were working *for the Lord*" (NLT, italics mine).

The Lifeline of God's Word

God has given each of you some special abilities; be sure to use them to help each other, passing on to others God's many kinds of blessings. Are you called to preach? Then preach as though God himself were speaking through you. Are you called to help others? Do it with all the strength and energy that God supplies, so that God will be glorified through Jesus Christ—to him be glory and power forever and ever.

1 Peter 4:10–11 TLB

Lord, thank you for the abilities and gifts you have given me. Help me to see these abilities as blessings that you want me to pass on to others. Deliver me from my fear of failure so I can use my talents with all the strength and energy that you want to supply, so you, God, will be glorified through Jesus Christ—to him be glory and power forever!

For I can do everything God asks me to with the help of Christ who gives me the strength and power.

Philippians 4:13 TLB

Lord, you who fills me with your dynamic power have made me able to cope with any challenge or situation. Help me remember that I can do everything you ask or call me to do with the help of Christ who gives me the strength and power! You have even said your power shows up best in weak people. Thank you for your plan for my life.

thirteen

Overcoming Fears Concerning Health

Faith is for that which lies on the other side of reason. Faith is what makes life bearable, with all of its tragedies and ambiguities and sudden, startling joys.

Madeleine L' Engle

God, why me?" asked Doris, lying alone in her hospital bed after she had received the diagnosis of terminal cancer. She had been a Christian for years and had loved and served God and her community for as long as she could remember; and she just didn't understand why she had to die of cancer. She had so much to do!

Doris's family had a long history of cancer: sisters, her mother, and even her husband just a few years before. As she lay there one night questioning God and asking him to heal her, she had a vision in her mind's eye. She saw herself standing before the cross holding something in her hand, and then she heard the

Lord say, "Doris, I can deal with the disease—the cancer—but I can't deal with the fear. That's yours to lay down." The Holy Spirit began to impress on her that she had harbored such a fear of cancer that her faith was literally paralyzed by her fears.

Suddenly, she saw herself take what was in her hands, put it in a box, tie a pink bow around it, and place it at the foot of the cross. Then she heard herself say aloud, "I lay all my fears about cancer, about dying, about my health at your feet, Jesus." Amazingly, when the doctors did her next CAT scan, every trace of the cancer was gone. She was restored to total health and lived many years after the incident.

Norman Cousins, author of *Anatomy of an Illness* and lay lecturer at many medical schools during his lifetime, said that many people die from their diagnosis rather than the disease. We do know that fear, anxiety, and panic affect us physically, and there is a strong connection between fear and illness, faith and healing. Fear consumes one's physical, mental, and spiritual energy, tearing down the very immune system God has provided to fight off infection and disease. And sometimes fearing a sickness can actually cause health problems and increase the likelihood of some illness afflicting or shortening your life, echoing in some sense Job's experience: "For what I fear comes upon me, and what I dread befalls me" (Job 3:25 NASB).

> When God allows extraordinary trials, He gives extraordinary comfort.
>
> *Unknown*

As Bruce Larson states in *Living beyond Our Fears,* "Fear has a somewhat magnetic quality I can't quite explain, but after a long lifetime of observing myself and others, I am convinced we are drawn to the very thing we fear the most. Our fears exert power over us. They often turn into self-fulfilling prophecies." He tells the story of a surgeon who shared one morning as their small group of men talked about their fears: "I fear two things," said the doctor. "I fear the loss of my skills as a surgeon, and I fear I will suffer from some condition whereby I will be unable to breathe. I have watched patients with that problem, and it is frightening." In only a year, the surgeon got both emphysema and arthritis, later suffered a stroke that deprived him the use of his right hand, and was forced to give up his practice. Like Doris, in a sense the doctor was drawn to the things he most feared.[1]

I have to admit that with parents dying relatively young, Papa at forty-seven of heart disease and Mama at fifty-nine of cancer, I've had some health concerns of my own, reflected in my statements like, "I don't worry about being put in a nursing home in my old age. Nobody in our family lives long enough to make it there." Or when my friends rush out and buy more decorations at half price the day after Christmas, I say, "I don't know if I'll even be here next Christmas." The first statement my niece Holly says is downright morbid, and after my fortieth and then forty-seventh birthdays, I realized the folly of the second statement, so I gave both those ideas and my fears to the Lord (and I do buy an occasional Christmas decoration a year ahead now!). For truly, only he knows how many years I'll be on earth before graduating to heaven.

The "Big C"

Sometimes, however, our fears are triggered by the bad news we receive from the doctor, a diagnosis that shatters our plans and changes our lives. On a June afternoon in 1991, Nancy, a forty-year-old wife and mother of two sons, was diagnosed with breast cancer. On that day, the "Big C" quickly swept in to take over her life, with its accompanying surgery, anxiety, hair loss, and pain. Because the cancer had spread into the bone of her neck and was at Stage 4, in a matter of five days she had a mastectomy and breast reconstruction surgery. She also began an aggressive round of chemotherapy and radiation treatments that would last for fourteen months.

After the doctor gave her the bleak statistics that there was only a 10 to 20 percent cure rate, with her chances for long-term recovery being very slim, she was overwhelmed by fear and about to dissolve in tears.

Driving home, she thought, *I can't cry yet; I might have a wreck. I'll wait until I get in the house to cry.* On the way into the house, she picked up her mail, and one of the top letters was from a ministry with a sketch of Daniel looking into the lions' den. A passage from 2 Chronicles 20:12 was written below with the words: "Fix your eyes on Jesus no matter what your circumstances!"

Nancy got out her Bible and first read the story of Daniel. Then she turned to 2 Chronicles to read the story of Jehoshaphat to find the connection. As she poured over the words, the whole chapter seemed to speak right to where she was, especially verse 12: "We are powerless . . . nor do we know what to do" (NASB). She spoke honestly to God: "Okay, Lord, I'm powerless against this cancer and don't know what to do, but I'm determined, just like Daniel did, just like Jehoshaphat did, to fix myself on you."

That attitude and determination—to fix her focus on God instead of the circumstances and the cancer—was the difference between life and death, between anxiety and peace for Nancy. She did finally sit down, begin to grieve, and have a good cry, but it wasn't in utter hopelessness. Only a few verses down, she read, "Go out and face the enemy and you will see the salvation of the Lord," giving her the determination to face her enemy, cancer, and do everything she had to do medically but to fix her eyes on God.

Several times Nancy had dreams about dying and dealt with her share of fear and worry. One of her greatest fears was that she would be "out of it" or lose function or the ability to speak and control herself. But as she continued focusing on God, time after time fear of the "Big C" was replaced by experiencing the Lord as her Comforter, Companion, and Counselor.

In the long battle with cancer she learned many things, the first being not to isolate herself because we become more afraid if we're alone. They had just moved to a new city and knew no one at the church they attended; it would have been easy to stay at home alone. But she found out there was a Tuesday morning ladies' Bible study and joined. There she got to know many women who prayed with her, cried with her when the chemotherapy caused depression and other side effects, and rejoiced with her when she had a good report. Her husband and teenage son also provided encouragement, support, and love.

Nancy also found that God meets each of us individually, walks with us through everything, and gives us what we need at precisely the time the grace is needed. While attending a workshop during one of her months of treatment, she met an older man whose wife had recently died of cancer. He shared with special compassion: "Either way, Nancy, you win. If you get well and recover from cancer, you win. If you die, you win because you get to be with Jesus." Her strength came from different sources. Sometimes it was a song playing on the CD when she was so lethargic after chemo she couldn't even read her Bible. One Sunday she was exhausted yet feeling like she had to keep herself "up" to conquer the mental struggles so she could stand strong. The special music was from Phil. 1:6, "He who began a good work in you will perfect it until the day of Christ" (NASB), and through it God was saying, "You don't have to do all the work yourself; I'm here with you, and I who began the good work in you will complete it!" Her part was to rest and abide in him.

> Few things will build intimacy with God as much as facing your fears with Him. (Our souls) will be knit to God when we learn to trust in Him alone, obeying His will even when we are afraid. After God leads me through a seemingly perilous situation, I'm all His. It's the most glorious, intimate fulfillment I've ever known.
>
> *Gary Thomas, Discipleship Journal*

The challenge, the choice, and the fight of faith for Nancy remains in keeping her eyes on Jesus. When she does, she's not afraid of the future or health problems, because she knows God will be with her and give her whatever she needs to get through it. He has walked her through a long wilderness to victory on the other side. And though she doesn't know the final outcome or what's ahead, she knows who holds her future.

Turning Points

Dr. Kay Toombs, assistant professor of philosophy at Baylor University, lives by the Viktor Frankl quote "Everything can be taken away from a person but the freedom to choose how to react to any given set of circumstances." She finds it incredibly freeing that no matter what happens to her body, she always has a choice as to how she responds.

In 1973, when Kay was first diagnosed with multiple sclerosis (MS), a degenerative disease of the central nervous system, she was not so confident. After suffering a temporary loss of vision in her right eye and receiving the diagnosis, her first reaction was to be absolutely terrified. She left the doctor's office and called the Multiple Sclerosis Society. At the first meeting she attended, they showed a movie about a man diagnosed with MS who within a matter of weeks was immobilized in a wheelchair while his wife was outside hammering up a "For Sale" sign.

She felt like that would be the blueprint for her life, which only increased her fears. For two years after her diagnosis, that movie colored her understanding of what it meant to have MS. Contemplating the grim prospects, she would go to sleep at night terrified that when she woke up, she wouldn't be able to move at all.

The turning point came after living with the disease for two years. She realized she could carry on with a relatively normal life with MS, but that she couldn't live with the paralyzing fear, because her fear was more debilitating than the illness. So she made conscious choices to focus on the present instead of worrying about what was going to happen to her and how her MS was going to progress in the future. For example, rather than thinking about what degree she was going to get or if she'd be well enough to finish her M.A., she focused on getting through the particular course she was enrolled in. By focusing on the present instead of fearing the future, she obtained not only two M.A.s but also a Ph.D.

One of the problems with serious illness is that people project all kinds of fears about the future. "What will I do if I can't get out of bed in five years and how will I deal with it? What if my illness progresses?" These "what if" fears turn into global anxiety about everything. Since the situation is in the future and you don't know how you would handle it, you can't deal with it, and your anxiety becomes an absolute loss of control.

Kay found three important keys to dealing with this anxiety: First, she focuses on the concrete difficulties instead of the imagined ones. For example, rather than worry that she may be so weak in the future that she can't teach her university classes, she has learned to focus on the real, concrete problem: How am I going to be able to stand at the podium to lecture for forty-five minutes? Then she looks for solutions: use an overhead projector, get a lift for her chair, etc.

Doing this, she discovered that once you solve the here and now problems, you gain a sense of control that takes away that global feeling of helplessness. This stops a lot of anxiety because you are accepting your condition and finding options for the difficulties but not letting fear paralyze you.

The whole notion of choice also drains away a lot of anxiety. What you are going to do with the time you have, how you are going to respond to the disease, choices in terms of medical treatment—it's very important to know you still have choices. For example, Kay underwent chemotherapy for four months but found it made her life so dysfunctional that it wasn't worth the little improvement. So she chose to stop the treatments.

Second, she found that often the things we fear the most don't turn out like we had imagined. After twenty-three years of living with MS, Kay has found that when we actually have to face what we have feared, it's not at all like we thought and usually not nearly as bad.

One of the most terrifying things to her was the thought that she would end up in a wheelchair. She wasted a lot of energy fearing being in a wheelchair. Kay is in a wheelchair now, and although she gets very irritated about how people respond to a person in a wheelchair, and although there are the frustrations of getting in and out of places, she still carries on with her life. She teaches at the university, does research, speaks at medical conferences, and does all the things she wanted to do. In addition to her role as a professor, she has published thirteen chapters and articles and authored several books, and she has spoken at the European Congress on Family Practice/Clinical Medicine in Sweden.

Third, Kay tries not to take herself too seriously. Humor allows her to see that difficult things have their amusing side. Blessed with a sense of humor, Kay looks for the light side, even in difficulties. Her lively sense of humor, typified by the sticker of the Muppet character, Kermit the Frog, on her motorized wheelchair, helps her keep a healthy perspective on things. And at the heart of her life and work is a commitment to live moment to moment, making the most of each day and each opportunity and anticipating the best.

Coping with the Challenges

When Kathy was pregnant with her fifth child, she found herself constantly ill with flu symptoms and extreme, debilitating fatigue. Finally, at seven months she insisted on having her blood sugar checked. The diagnosis: diabetes. They also discovered her out-of-control blood sugar posed a danger to the health of their baby. Insulin shots got her through the pregnancy, and their baby was born without birth defects or complications.

During those last eight weeks she was told the diabetes might go away after the delivery, so Kathy set her worries aside. She didn't want to face the fact that this could be a chronic condition. But after her baby was born, she found out she had Type II diabetes, and she was overwhelmed. She couldn't escape reality—diabetes was going to be with her for the rest of her life.

In the beginning when her blood sugar was difficult to control, she was filled with fears about the future, about possible complications the doctor had warned her about such as damage to her eyesight or heart. The fears she experienced caused a high anxiety level; and because stress raises blood sugar levels, that in turn caused her sugar to rage out of control. Somehow she had to come to grips with her chronic illness *and* her anxiety. Out of this challenge she found her foundation and bedrock needed to be relying on and trusting in the sovereignty of God. She chose to rest in the knowledge of who God is (which hadn't changed just because she had diabetes) and in his ultimate control over all that occurred in her life. Establishing a daily, intimate walk with him, she began moment by moment to surrender to his plan.

This didn't come easily for Kathy—it was a yearlong process. Like Jacob in the Old Testament, she is a wrestler by nature. She did a lot of wrestling with God over the "whys" and "ifs"—"If God has the power to prevent this, why didn't he?"—and she wrestled with guilt—"What did I do to cause this?"

Finally she relinquished control of her life and the diabetes, realizing that even if the diabetes appeared to be negative in her life, the Lord has promised to use everything, even diabetes, for her good and his glory. His love became her anchor, and she rested in the truth of Romans 8:35–39, that nothing could remove her from the love of Christ, including illness: "Neither death nor life, neither angels nor demons, neither the present nor the future, nor any powers, neither height nor depth, nor anything else in all creation, will be able to separate us from the love of God that is in Christ Jesus our Lord."

Becoming knowledgeable about the illness empowered Kathy to do her part responsibly while letting go of those aspects in which she could not effect control. At times she does all that is required medically yet still experiences high, out-of-control blood sugar levels. To gain more knowledge, she looked for book and magazine resources and tapped into the experiences of people facing the same illness and people with medical expertise. The choice of a physician helped relieve much of her anxiety. A chronic illness demands a long-term relationship. By knowing herself and what was important to her in a doctor-patient "fit," Kathy found a doctor who showed respect and sensitivity for her desires and concerns.

Looking for and enjoying the simple pleasures of daily life helped her get her joy back. She found she can't always control the quality of her life, but she can determine its fullness. So she purposefully creates beauty in her surroundings, invests herself passionately in her relationships of family and friends, enjoys and celebrates daily life with her children, and takes time to nurture herself in areas of personal interests and hobbies.

From Fear to Faith

The fear of illness and the reality of diagnosis can be anxiety producing for anyone. How can we respond in a way that neutralizes those fears and keeps us in the ongoing process of wholeness?

Don't assume it's an automatic death sentence if you are diagnosed with breast cancer, heart disease, or another serious illness. And whenever there is a medical problem or negative diagnosis in your family, see that although it is a possibility for you, God is the final authority. If your mother or grandmother suffered with cancer, a stroke, or cardiac problems years ago, remember that great strides in treatment have been made. Take your diagnosis and lay it at the altar, asking God for his wisdom, direction for treatment, and hope.

> Whatever illness you're facing right now, your own or that of a loved one, keep in mind that God, not your doctor, *has* the last word. Through God we have unlimited resources to continue to live abundantly and generously all our remaining days, be they many or few.
>
> *Bruce Larson,*
> Living beyond Our Fears

If you are afraid of suffering with an illness or disease, bring those fears to God in prayer, pray about them with a trusted friend or pastor as well, and ask God to free you from the dread and anxiety as he shows you the roots behind your fear.

When there is a diagnosis or new information, hold it up to the light of Scripture. For example, when the doctors told Nancy her medications and chemotherapy could adversely affect her heart, Nancy looked up and meditated on many Scriptures about the heart such as "A cheerful heart is good medicine" (Prov. 17:22) and "Comfort and strengthen your hearts in every good work and word" (2 Thess. 2:17 NASB). Find Scriptures you can call your own and add to your Peace Packet to remind you that God knows your problem and will work in your situation.

And in the final analysis, as each of these women realized, it is wise to pray for healing and to appropriate all the grace and truth God provides in Scripture, while at the same time employing all the resources medical science has to offer and doing our part to care for our bodies. But the final outcome is with God, whether our healing is on this side or is the ultimate healing in heaven.

Don't waste your troubles but reach out to others. My friend Lisbeth took 2 Corinthians 1:3–4, "Praise be to the God and Father of our Lord Jesus Christ, the Father of compassion and the God of all comfort, who comforts us in all our troubles, so that we can comfort those in any trouble with the comfort we ourselves have received from God," to say that what she went through in her double mastectomy and chemotherapy over twenty years ago would have been wasted if she hadn't used her experience to reach out and share help with others. So she kept a Gratefulness Journal and every day wrote down things people did that helped her: a verse she was given, flowers that arrived, the small pillow, the special hat someone brought her. Later she had her dressmaker make similar hats, which she gives to friends who go through cancer. Remembering the kindness and comfort she received has helped her pass out buckets of comfort to others.

Since her recovery, Lisbeth has reached out to over 200 women with cancer. She not only has a list of their names and addresses in her Daytimer so she can send them cards at Christmas and other times, she also keeps blank journals on hand and takes one when she visits someone diagnosed with cancer. She encourages them to write in it every day, starting with a simple list of helps: the phone call at just the right time when you were feeling down; the card your son sent you; the Scripture that lifted your heart. She tells them that on the days that are really rough, they can look in their journal and see how God has worked, and it will help them pass on kindness to others.

Lisbeth started a "Bosom Buddies" support group for women battling or surviving cancer. They meet for lunch once a month. They chat, laugh, and share things that have worked in their own lives. One month Lisbeth took Jan, a new friend who was feeling particularly low after surgery and losing her hair due to chemotherapy, to lunch. Jan wondered if it would ever grow back or if she would ever feel good again. When Jan walked in and saw the whole tableful of women, she said, "I never would have guessed that the common bond of this table of beautiful women was breast cancer—they were happy and laughing. They had been through cancer too, were living productive lives—and their hair had grown back!" Being a part of that group was a significant factor in Jan's recovery.

Kay Toombs has found her firsthand experience of chronic illness combined with her philosophical training positioned her uniquely to teach and write on issues related to the challenges of incurable illness and to impact the practice of hundreds of physicians across the country and world to better care for the chronically or terminally ill. And Nancy not only led small support groups for women going through cancer and serious illness but wrote a devotional to inspire them.

Learn to ask for help from other people and from God. When Stacey, a single woman in her thirties, was blindsided by cancer, she discovered she had to lay down her pride and learn to ask for help. She was very independent and self-sufficient, so this wasn't easy at first. But she discovered there are resources out there—community resources, support groups, church, Bible studies, and friends that can help, but asking and being willing to accept help is a key. Sometimes she didn't have the energy to take chemotherapy while keeping up with a challenging job, paying bills, and taking care of her household. Sometimes she just needed extra hands.

Also, she learned to allow God to be what he promises. He promises he'll be your comfort; he'll hold you up; he'll provide for your needs. Stacey knew she was already his child. All she had to do was to appropriate his promises. In receiving God's help and learning to lean on him, she experienced a kind of peace and intimacy with the Lord she had never had before.

Lifelines from God's Word

May the God of hope fill you with all joy and peace as you trust in him, so that you may overflow with hope by the power of the Holy Spirit.

Romans 15:13

Lord, fill me with hope, joy, and peace and help me to trust in you! Encompass me with your loving arms and enable me to overflow with hope by the power of your Holy Spirit. Here are the fears I have regarding illness or disease . . .

Surely He has borne our griefs (sicknesses, weaknesses, and distresses) and carried our sorrows and pains . . . But He was wounded for our transgressions, He was bruised for our guilt and iniquities; the chastisement [needful to obtain] peace and well-being for us was upon Him, and with the stripes [that wounded] Him we are healed and made whole.

Isaiah 53:4–5 AMP

Lord, thank you for bearing our griefs, weaknesses, and distresses. In the midst of my illness, thank you for carrying my sorrow and pain. Thank you that you are the Great Physician and Jehovah Rapha, the Lord My Healer, and I can come to you with all the things I suffer. Help me to trust you in health as well as in affliction. I ask for your healing power and presence to fill my body, my soul, and my spirit.

fourteen

Overcoming Fears in the Midst of Disaster

Have no fear of sudden disaster or of the ruin that overtakes the wicked, for the LORD will be your confidence and will keep your foot from being snared.

Proverbs 3:25–26

The headlines of the past few years are full of disasters and calamities: In addition to the terrorist attacks around the world, there have been sniper shootings around Washington, D.C., widespread floods throughout Europe, war in Iraq, and dangerous wildfires here and abroad. It's enough to cause some people to avoid watching the news or stop reading newspapers. We live in an increasingly violent world, and anxiety about disasters is on the rise—fear about those uncontrollable, huge events that crash into our lives and change things forever.

"I can handle the day-to-day struggles like sickness and financial problems, my husband not paying child support, or losing the house," a woman said recently. "But I couldn't handle a major disaster. I don't know if my faith could stand that kind of test, and I don't know if I could survive the tragedy."

Many storms in life are uncontrollable, says Larry Jones of Feed the Children Ministry. Larry has seen some of the worst disasters in the twentieth century: the famine in Ethiopia, the war in Bosnia, the torrential floods of the Midwest, Hurricane Gilbert that destroyed much of the island of Jamaica. And his ministry, Feed the Children, has been there to deliver help with planeloads of food, medical supplies, and clothes.

> Fear. His modus operandi is to manipulate you with the mysterious, to taunt you with the unknown.
>
> Max Lucado,
> Travelling Light

"Stormy marriages, financial storms, physical storms like cancer, stormy plagues like AIDS," he says, "we can't always avoid or prevent them. But we can control the way we respond to them. If we control our reaction, we can tap into God's provision and ride out the storm in peace."[1]

But what about when the uncontrollable comes crashing into *our* lives unexpectedly? And what happens to already anxious worriers when real disaster strikes? Is God able to sustain us?

Cyndi and Steve were the happy parents of two sons, ages ten and six, and were awaiting the birth of their first daughter when disaster struck their lives in December of 1991. Steve was on his way to Sunday school one morning when he was hit head-on by a teenage drunk driver. Taken to Mercy Health Center with a severe brain injury, he was not expected to live past twenty-four hours. For five months, Steve lay in a coma. He saw nothing, heard nothing, and did nothing. Repeatedly the neurosurgeon said, "I see no significant change."

Normally Cyndi wasn't a worrier. She could get stressed-out over grades in college, but temperamentally, she is laid-back. But with her husband in a life-threatening condition, the doctors only giving him a fair chance to make it, and medical bills mounting for critical care, she was filled with fear about some very big, very real issues: *Will my husband ever recover? How am I going to have this baby by myself, without Steve? How can I go through delivery alone? Am I going to have to put this newborn in day care and go to work? And how are we going to make it financially?*

Her first challenges were single parenting and being at the hospital with Steve for countless hours while in her last stage of pregnancy. One day she was given a devastating report that Steve's condition was deteriorating and he could be in the coma indefinitely. A visiting pastor told her, "We don't always get a miracle." That night was one of her darkest nights. She couldn't sleep and knew she could easily be lost in a pit of fear and worry.

Choosing to Believe

As she walked up and down the stairs at Mercy Hospital the next day, words from Jeremiah 29:11 went through her mind: "'For I know the plans that I have for you,' declares the LORD, 'plans for welfare and not for calamity to give you a future and a hope'" (NASB). That verse kept flashing on the screen of her mind.

> **Put your powerlessness in God's almighty power, and find in waiting on God your deliverance.**
>
> *Andrew Murray*

"You believed this before the accident and you've stood on that truth for minor circumstances. It's still true now," God seemed to say to her, encouraging her to believe in him and his Word, regardless of what the circumstances looked like before or after the head-on crash. "Do you believe I am who I say I am?"

Cyndi chose to believe and persisted each day no matter how things looked on the outside. Regardless of where they ended up, she was convinced that Scripture was still true, that there was a future for her and her family and good for their lives ahead. Holding on to that truth helped her keep up her hope and stay out of the pit of anxiety. From then on, although they faced many daily struggles, some of them overwhelming, she didn't struggle with feeling abandoned or bitter. She had some real worries about the upcoming birth and finances and one of the biggest issues—how she was going to raise her boys without a father, if necessary.

Cyndi and her family's experience is a good example of the principle that 98 percent of what we worry about doesn't come true. The other 2 percent that comes true we can't control anyway.

Her daughter, Katelyn, was delivered in a warm family atmosphere with twenty-five friends and family in the waiting room, cheering her on and celebrating. A great female OB-Gyn and three friends served as the best labor and delivery team she could have hoped for. She was definitely not alone!

Her baby was certainly God's gift; but as they went home from the hospital, Cyndi had to face her fear of having to put her in day care and work. Initially she wasn't worried about finances. She was just making it from day to day by focusing on her husband's survival. But when her husband emerged from the coma five months after the accident, she was faced with a new bundle of worries. One of these hit her the day she was being shown the rehabilitation unit that Steve would be put into for an indefinite number of months. All of a sudden, the bleakness and severity of what they were facing hit home.

"Here's where we'll show him how to open a can, so that eventually when he's at home alone while you're working, he can fix something to eat," the social worker said.

God's Provision

Upon hearing their fate, Cyndi sat down at the table and wept. She didn't know how she could put her infant in day care and support the family while taking care of a disabled husband. But in actuality, this fear never materialized. In March a former client of Steve's had a fund-raiser and in one day raised $7,000. The Radio Council held an auction and made $17,000. Their church started a fund that went on for three and a half years, and people contributed thousands of dollars to their family's support. Every step of the way God took care of them. It was a great lesson for Cyndi on not borrowing worry from the future; besides, she needed her energy to take care of each day's challenges. But day by day, God's grace was there.

It was just like the help the Lord brought in the midst of a famine to a widow who was on the way home carrying only a few sticks so she could cook what she had for herself and her son, and afterward, starve to death. Elijah said to her:

> "Don't be afraid. Go home and do as you have said. But first make a small cake of bread for me from what you have and bring it to me, and then make something for yourself and your son. For this is what the LORD, the God of Israel, says: 'The jar of flour will not be used up and the jug of oil will not run dry until the day the LORD gives rain on the land.'"
>
> 1 Kings 17:13–14

She went away and did as Elijah had told her. And sure enough, her family had food enough for a long time. She never ran out of oil or flour until the famine ended. In a similar way, the funds raised for Cyndi's family lasted right up until the settlement from the insurance company was finalized. Even though Steve had been hospitalized for twenty-two months and had been unable to earn an income, his family was debt free.

And though Steve was now uninsurable and in a wheelchair, unable to ever work in a full-time job, Cyndi didn't worry about how they were going to make it financially. God had been too faithful for her to fall into fear. And the God who spoke to her on the stairs of the hospital, saying, "I still have a future and a hope for you," is the same God who carried them when two years later, right before they were to move into the new wheelchair-accessible house that was built for them, Steve was diagnosed with leukemia and died only a few days later. He is the same God Cyndi trusted several years later when she married Mike, a pastor at her church whose wife had died of cancer, as they blended their families and kept their kids afloat. Cyndi's remarkable story is told in her book, *Keeping Your Kids Afloat When You Feel Like You're Sinking.*

How did Cyndi survive such a series of tragedies in her life and family? By gaining a bigger picture and an eternal perspective, or as Amy Carmichael called it, "looking from the top."

A Bigger Picture

When a devastating situation hits our lives, we can feel like we're on the bottom, overwhelmed by the circumstances—not "on top of things" like we'd like to be. If you get caught in the crush of life and pushed down, says Amy Carmichael in *Edges of His Ways*, "the next thing we know is that we are groveling in the dust. Things are on the top of *us*, we are not on the top of anything."

So God calls us to "look from the top" (Song of Sol. 4:8).

Come with Me from all that, come up the mountain with Me, and look from the top. In everyday life this simply means, look from everything up to the Lord Jesus, Who is our Peace, our Victory, and our Joy, *for we are where we look*. From below, things feel impossible, people seem impossible (some people at least), and we ourselves feel most impossible of all. From the top we see as our Lord sees; He sees not what *is* only, but what shall be. He is not discouraged, and as we look with Him, our discouragement vanishes, and we can sing a new song.[2]

As Steve and Cyndi found out, bad things happen to everyone. Just ask Jesus. He came into the painful world we live in and wasn't spared problems. Part of their big picture was understanding that, as Steve said, "Though we think life is supposed to be a smooth road with little pockets of interruptions, trials, and change, the truth is life is a road full of change and difficulties with little pockets of serenity." And part of why Christians are here, we believe, is to show the world how to solve problems, even seemingly insurmountable ones, with Christ.

When Lisa Beamer's husband, Todd, died in the ill-fated Flight 93 hijacked by terrorists on September 11, 2001, her bigger picture, her focus on God, enabled her to experience a peace that mystified the media and inspired a nation: "Probably the most important truth," said Lisa, "is that my security must be in *God* rather than in anything or anyone in this world."[3] That day the symbols of power and security, the World Trade Center and the Pentagon, were destroyed and shaken. Faced with the impending birth of their daughter and raising their two sons alone in the midst of great uncertainty and loss, Lisa had to deal with the question, "Where can we find true security in these days?"

"I have found safety and security in a loving heavenly Father, who cannot be shaken, who will never leave me or forsake me, and in whom I can trust completely," Lisa said.[4]

We are all bound to face some storm, tragedy, or crisis that seems uncontrollable and not of our choosing. By getting our own big picture perspective on life, we will realize and experience, as Lisa did, that the Lord is our only source of safety and security.

Changed Forever

Part of the amazing thing about God is how he can use even the worst of situations the enemy meant for destruction and evil to transform both the situation and our own lives and hearts. He can turn terrible trials into trust builders, and even calamities into a new confidence and trust in him. With the Lord's awesome presence and power in the midst of our crisis, he can actually *deliver us* from fear as we move through the situation so that we emerge more whole, healthy individuals. That's what happened when disaster struck Priscilla Salyers's life.

When she pushed the door open to her office at the U.S. Customs office on the fifth floor of the Murrah Federal Building the morning of April 19, 1995, she had no idea that her life and the lives of her coworkers and friends would be changed forever. After picking up the mail on the first floor earlier than she had in seven years and visiting with her friend Paul Ice over coffee, she went to her desk to begin work.

Moments later, as she picked up the phone, a blast like a huge sonic boom shook the building and suddenly everything went black. Priscilla was picked up by a huge whirlwind. Flashes of light like stars swirled around her. Wind roared in her ears and she lost control of her body.

When everything stopped, she felt a massive jolt and couldn't move anything except for her left arm. What she didn't know is that a huge truck bomb had destroyed the Federal Building, and she had fallen all the way from the fifth floor to below the first floor, into what was later called "The Pit." She was trapped face-down under concrete and rubble.

As the heaviness of silence sunk in, Priscilla prayed two things: "Lord, keep me calm, and give me the wisdom for survival." As she kept praying those words, she remembered how earthquake victims who survived had made it three days—because they found an air pocket to breathe. With her left hand, she dug out some rubble from under her neck to create an air pocket. Only then could she breathe, but it took every ounce of strength and concentration she had.

Finally rescuers found her and a man closed his hand over hers. All her worries transferred to his hand—it was like God's hand extended to her. Such peace and safety she felt. But that respite was short-lived, for soon the man said, "Priscilla, we have to leave."

Panic swept through her and she gripped his hand tighter, begging him not to go, "Please don't leave me! Don't leave me . . ."

What she didn't know was that a second bomb threat caused a forced evacuation of the entire building. The second silence was worse than the first. For four hours she lay there alone—sometimes hyperventilating, several times desperately wanting to fall asleep.

After what seemed an eternity, Priscilla could hear movement and voices in the distance. She pounded on the surface next to her so they wouldn't miss her. Then she heard a voice say, "We've got a live one down here," as someone took her hand. That same comforting, peaceful feeling she'd had before filled her again.

Rescuers worked with chain saws and the Jaws of Life to lift the concrete and rubble off Priscilla and eventually to free her body. As they carried her out on a spinal board, she saw her first sight in hours—the blue sky above. To her left it looked like a war zone, and she knew then the entire building was devastated. After five days in the hospital, where her broken ribs, collapsed lung, and other injuries were treated, Priscilla came home to an emotional welcome from her husband, two sons, family, and friends. In the midst of pain, she was preoccupied with two questions: *God, what do you expect of me now—how can I put my life back together?* and *Why didn't Mickey, Paul, and the other Christians make it? Why, God?*

Sitting up in a recliner that first night after everyone had gone to bed, Priscilla opened the Bible and read Romans 12. Present your body to God, the passage said. Whatever gifts you have, use them for others and do it well . . . really love people and even invite them home for dinner. Don't repay evil for evil (she knew then God would take care of those who bombed the building; she didn't have to hold bitterness against them). She saw clearly that God was not expecting her to do fantastic works, but if she lived the way he described here, then the purpose she survived for would be fulfilled.

He Rescued Them

The next day when she attended her good friend Mickey Maroney's memorial service in a wheelchair, she was still asking, *Why, God? Why didn't he make it? He was so devoted to you.*

"This poor man cried, and the LORD heard him, and saved him out of all his troubles. The angel of the LORD encamps around those who fear Him, and rescues them" (Ps. 34:6–7 NASB) was the first verse read. As that truth sunk in, it hit her—*He did rescue them. He took them home!*

Then her mind flashed back to how he had been with her: Jesus' presence in the bombed building when she was buried under concrete. When the rescuer held her hand, it was Jesus' hand. His Spirit reminding her to breathe slowly and keep calm so she could get air in the small space. Jesus' presence surrounded her in the hospital and in the outpouring of comfort from friends and people all over the country, many she didn't even know. Wherever Priscilla had been, Jesus was with her. She suddenly knew the Lord was also with those who died, sending angels to care for them and take them to heaven. She knew God would be with her in the long recovery that lay ahead and that he had a purpose for the rest of her life.

God's nearness in the face of death was so real that Priscilla doesn't fear death anymore. His peace was so overwhelming that she knows when it's time for her to join Paul, Claude, and her other friends who died, she won't fear, for Jesus will be with her. This peace sustained her during months of pain and grieving and brought her into more freedom than she had ever known. Before the bombing, she was very timid and never spoke before a group, not even a small one. But a few weeks after the tragedy, a church service was held for the paramedics, who were struggling with guilt about not saving more people than they did.

She knew there was something she needed to tell those paramedics, but at first she thought, *Not me*. All her life she had been too scared to get up in front of a group. She hadn't even gone into a church for ages but felt God's leading to be there and share her experience. "Lord, give me the words," she prayed. That night as she faced over seventy-five rescuers, she told them about the incredible peace she had when the fireman was holding her hand, that for every person they touched, they gave a priceless gift—they were God's hand extended to them in either their last moments or until they were rescued.

Before, Priscilla had been too shy and afraid to share Christ but never again. She was no longer ashamed to let anybody know that God brought her through and to share the good news about Christ. Countless people have been given hope by her story.

From Fear to Faith

Whether you are afraid of a potential disaster or find yourself in the midst of a calamity, you can move from fear to a confident faith. Just as Cyndi, Lisa, and Priscilla found, you can experience God's peace in the midst of a storm by the following:

Being anchored in his love. What helped Cyndi more than anything else in the crisis she faced was that before going into it, she had *a deep belief that God loved her.* That foundation didn't come easily; in fact, as a young Christian she struggled with believing God loved her because she came from a divorced family with a faithless, alcoholic father who couldn't be depended on.

But a youth leader who knew of Cyndi's struggle encouraged her to pray every single day, "Lord, teach me that you love me." Throughout her twenties and early thirties, she continued praying that prayer each day, and she found herself consistently discovering how much he loved her. As a result, God's love became a real anchor in her life. That's a prayer he loves to answer. And believing in his love for you is an undergirding truth. If you internalize it, not only in your head but in your heart, it will help you face any difficulty or crisis with more faith and less anxiety.

You must really know in your gut that whatever happens, God loves you and has the best interests of you, your spouse (if you have one), and your children at heart—ultimately he has a plan that he will see accomplished—a plan for "a future filled with hope," as Jeremiah 29:11 describes. Armed with this belief, you don't have to waste your energy fighting God or the circumstances. The "whys" might come to visit, but they don't have to take up residence. If you constantly struggle with knowing God loves you and can't identify with this kind of belief in God's care and love, you can still pray this prayer even in the darkest moment: "I want to believe that you love me and I want to believe your Word. Would you show me and teach me about your love?"

Sensing his presence. God's promise is that he will be with us. From the time that we become his children through believing in Jesus Christ, his presence indwells us and his care for us is secure, just as it was for Priscilla. Since God is our true environment and dwelling place, and we're surrounded by his care each moment of the day, we can know that wherever we are and whatever may happen, he is with us and within us. The Christian is guarded on all sides by the Lord. We have God before us (Isa. 48:17), God behind us (Isa. 30:21), God on our right (Ps. 16:8), God to our left (Job 23:9), God above us (Ps. 36:7), God's arms underneath us (Deut. 33:27), and his Spirit within us (1 Cor. 6:19).[5]

God himself has said, "I will not in any way fail you nor give you up nor leave you without support. [I will] not. [I will] not, [I will] not in any degree leave you helpless nor forsake nor let [you] down (relax My hold on you)! Assuredly not!" (Heb. 13:5 AMP).

But although God is with us, we often don't sense his presence or realize he's there. Just like the disciples didn't recognize Jesus when he came to them on the water in the midst of the storm, when we're in a dark place we may feel he hasn't

> **Be assured, if you walk with Him and look to Him and expect help from Him, He will never fail you.**
>
> *George Mueller*

shown up. When that happens and you feel left alone, pray that God will open your eyes and heart to see what he's doing, to sense his presence in the midst of the storm, and to know the truth—that he is with you.

Even though Heather Mercer and Dayna Curry were aware of God's presence, there were times during their imprisonment in Afghanistan while bombs were exploding around the prison, while they were being interrogated for hours, that they experienced worry and fear. "After the September 11 attacks on America, and then again after the U.S. started bombing Kabul, I had to regroup," Dayna explained. "I asked myself, 'What if I die?' I determined to believe in God's goodness." In prison she said, "Okay, Lord, I believe You're good. I trust that if I die right now in this situation, it must be the best thing for me. If I die, I'll be with You. If dying will cause many people to call upon Jesus, then dying would be an honor." She added, "Of course, I really didn't want to die. I wanted the chance to get married, to have a family. I didn't believe I was going to die based on what the Lord seemed to be saying to me; but I accepted death as a possibility, and I didn't fear it. I trusted the Lord with my life." Ultimately, that step is one we all have to take regardless of our circumstances.[6]

Personalizing his promises. Personalizing God's promises for protection will remind you that your safety and security is in the Lord. Memorize these faith-filled verses and say them aloud:

You are my hiding place!
You protect me from trouble,
and You put songs in my heart
because You have saved me.

Psalm 32:7 THE PROMISE

The Lord will protect you and keep you safe from all dangers.
The Lord will protect you now and always wherever you go.

Psalm 121:7–8 THE PROMISE

Live under the protection of God Most High
and stay in the shadow of God All-Powerful.
Then you will say to the Lord,
"You are my fortress, my place of safety;
you are my God, and I trust You."

Psalm 91:1–2 THE PROMISE

Focusing on today. You can overcome the fear that something disastrous might happen by focusing on today, not worrying about and projecting on tomorrow's future troubles—instead put your efforts and energy into what God has put on your plate today. Jesus told us not to worry about tomorrow (Luke 12:29), not to let our hearts be troubled (John 14:1).

We tend to borrow from tomorrow's troubles and thus not have enough energy to focus on what we are called to do with the present day we are given. As Sir John Lubbock said, "A day of worry is more exhausting than a day of work." Resist the urge to "catastrophize" or frighten yourself with your own thoughts about the worst that can happen.

"When we fuel our fears by catastrophizing, we actually create mental anguish and become our own worst enemy," says Pam Vredevelt, licensed professional counselor and author of *Letting Go.* "The good news is that we don't have to compulsively follow every train of thought that enters our head . . . If we do, our imaginations can run wild, and the more we do, the more anxious we feel. It's a vicious spiral. But the spiral can be easily interrupted. We can say *stop* to our thoughts."[7]

If you refuse to assume the worst, resist the fearful thoughts, replace them with faith-filled truths, and focus on today, you will discover a new strength and hope to deal with each day's challenges.

Serving someone else. One of the ways Priscilla has found healing is to reach out to others—from the first group of paramedics she shared with to other people in churches to whom she has given hope and inspiration. She also reached out to the grieving families of Paul and Claude, her closest coworkers who died in the bombing, and every other week she got together with a small group of survivors for dinner. They had all lost friends, family, or coworkers and were all dealing with pain. But being together, talking, and helping each other aided the healing process. Becoming isolated and preoccupied with self only increases fear and anxiety.

"There is no greater cure for our personal fears than to help others in need," says Don Gossett. "Victorious saints of God are persons who, though human and prone to fear, spend themselves in service and thus have no time for worry."[8]

Find someone to encourage and help—a single parent who needs assistance, a child in need of support, an elderly person who is a shut-in due to ill health. Don't wait until your problems are solved to help someone else. Do what God has called you to today. When you spend yourselves in sharing God's love by serving others, you'll experience a new sense of his peace.

Lifelines from God's Word

Praying God's Word back to him, remembering that he is our Protector, dispels fear wherever we are—in a storm, a bombing, an airplane, or on a highway—and reminds us that our safety is in the Lord.

I have set the LORD always before me. Because he is at my right hand, I will not be shaken. Therefore my heart is glad and my tongue rejoices.

Psalm 16:8–9

God is our refuge and strength, an ever-present help in trouble. Therefore we will not fear, though the earth give way and though the mountains fall into the heart of the sea; though its waters roar and foam and the mountains quake with their surging.

Psalm 46:1–3

Lord, you hold me in the palm of your hand. You surround me and your Spirit dwells within me; therefore, though everything may be shaken, I will not be shaken, because you hold me securely. You are my refuge and strength, an ever-present help in trouble. Therefore, I won't fear, though the earth give way or the mountains fall into the sea. You are God, my security on this earth and my eternal security.

Now the Lord who created you, O Israel, says, Don't be afraid, for I have ransomed you; I have called you by name; you are mine. When you go through deep waters and great trouble, I will be with you. When you go through rivers of difficulty, you will not drown! When you walk through the fire of oppression, you will not be burned up—the flames will not consume you. For I am the Lord your God, your Savior, the Holy One of Israel . . . You are precious to me and honored, and I love you. Don't be afraid, for I am with you.

Isaiah 43:1–5 TLB

I may walk through valleys as dark as death, but I won't be afraid. You are with me, and your shepherd's rod makes me feel safe.

Psalm 23:4 THE PROMISE

Lord, though I walk through dark valleys, I won't be afraid. You are with me. Though I go through deep waters and great trouble, you have promised to be with me. You are the Lord my God. Thank you that you love me and I don't have to be afraid, for you are with me; you make me feel safe. Thank you, Father, for your loving care, your protection, and your faithfulness!

epilogue

Living the Adventure

The initial call to discipleship was a call to adventure. The early disciples were called to leave their families and the comfort and security of familiar ways and places, to go they knew not where, and to do they knew not what. Day by day they discovered that life was a great adventure, and that every hardship and every setback was a doorway to new service and maturity.

Keith Miller and Bruce Larson

One Sunday night in 1978 after a small group meeting, a woman in the group approached Holmes and me.

"You really seem to believe all that," she observed.

"All what?" I asked. "The material we discussed tonight?"

"No, I mean you really believe the Bible is true, don't you? You seem to be applying this stuff—like it's not just a myth or story but something you can build your whole life on," she added.

"Yes, we really do. That's what makes life so exciting," I answered.

For us, the adventure had begun. Layer by layer, God was helping me face my fears, transforming us through his Spirit. Our marriage began to change. Our priorities changed. As we kept pursuing God, both our careers changed. But the biggest change of all was that we found life a day-by-day adventure and that God had a different purpose for us than what we had planned.

I don't believe the Lord saves us and brings us out of darkness into his marvelous light, delivers us from our fears, and fills us with his Spirit so we can stay in our comfort zones and feel peaceful and secure. Instead, I think he wants to move us beyond our fears to a transformation of our inner being and a passionate pursuit of his purpose for our lives. As Paul said, in following Jesus we are "transformed . . . from glory to glory, just as by the Spirit of the Lord" (2 Cor. 3:18 NKJV). Following Jesus won't always be comfortable—changes can be scary and uncertain, and difficulties and trials may come our way on the journey. At times new challenges or situations may be frightening. But if we start living life as the great adventure God means it to be, then every difficulty, every obstacle can be the door to purpose, life, and growth.

> **Do not despise this small beginning . . .**
>
> *Zechariah 4:10 (TLB)*

"Like ancient Israel, God created us to be a spiritually nomadic people who travel light along life's journey as we pursue the pillar of fire, the cloud of glory and the ark of His presence. We were created for the journey, not just for the destination," said Terry Crist.[1]

Here are some of the principles we have learned along the way that have helped us continue the journey and live life as a great adventure with Christ:

Show up for service! When you present yourself as a living sacrifice like Romans 12:1 directs, be ready for the adventure to accelerate, for God is looking for willing vessels. "For the eyes of the LORD range throughout the earth to strengthen those whose hearts are fully committed to him," says 2 Chronicles 16:9.

We are the vessels—not perfect ones but willing ones. "But we have this treasure in earthen vessels, that the surpassing greatness of the power may be of God and not from ourselves" (2 Cor. 4:7 PHILLIPS).

Showing up for service also means connecting with God each morning, before the day crushes in on us with its tasks, e-mails, phone calls, and carpooling, to surrender anew—with a heart saying, "Here's my life, my hands, my emotions and will, my intellect—all that I am. Use me today in whatever way you want. Give me a specific word of encouragement for someone who needs it. Show me how I can serve, help, comfort someone. No matter how small the task, here I am—use me!" The specific words don't matter as much as turning to God in whatever way helps you yield and give yourself and your day to him.

As you give yourself to him with what Oswald Chambers called "a reckless abandon,"[2] you will begin to find the purpose or mission you were created for doing in this particular season of your life. You may need some more training or preparation. But whether it is painting pictures, programming computers, administrating a business or ministry, teaching and nurturing children, inventing something new, dancing or singing or composing music—he has gifted you and equipped you to fulfill the very purpose for which he made you.

Take one step at a time. When you know what your interests or gifts are, what you enjoy doing, or what God is calling you to (i.e., what you are passionate about), then it's time to begin following the guidance he gives you. Psalm 119:105 says his Word *will* light our path. It's a promise! When God shows you a step to take and you take it, he will give you the light you need for the next step. I find he rarely reveals the whole blueprint—more often he reveals the next step in his plan.

Paul writes, "For we are His workmanship, created in Christ Jesus for good works, which God prepared beforehand so that we would walk in them" (Eph. 2:10 NASB). He has planned things for you and me to do—ahead of time, before we ever thought about them! I believe there are songs in heaven God is looking for someone to write, stories he wants told, missionary projects he has in mind, inner-city tutoring programs to help at-risk kids. He doesn't have problems, just plans! He has already thought of them in heaven and wants willing vessels to accomplish them on earth.

But just like a miner's hat, which casts a beam six feet ahead to give enough light to illuminate his next steps, until we take the step and walk those six feet, we won't be able to see more of the path. Taking the steps often involves risk. In fact, someone said that "faith" is spelled "R-I-S-K." And it doesn't matter what your age or stage of life; if you follow his light, amazing things will happen.

One day Louise Montgomery was waiting for her car to be repaired in a small town in Maine, when into the auto shop strolled Alison Kelley, and the two women, who had never met, began chatting. Soon they discovered that although they were twenty years apart in age, they had much in common, especially that both were strong believers in the power of prayer. The two became prayer partners.

Alison, a registered nurse, often spoke to Louise about her volunteer work at a shelter for the homeless in Boston. As they talked and prayed, Louise became convinced God wanted her to open a shelter in Portland.

And so, by following the guidance God was giving her, Louise and her husband, both in their mid-seventies, took their life savings of $50,000 and began combing Portland for a big house. "You'll never find a house for that money," real estate agents told them. "You're too old to do something this huge," others said.

But God had given Louise a dream and a mission, and find a house they did—a fourteen-room dilapidated structure. Restoring it was a huge project, but as she prayed Louise felt directed to ask for help from the Cumberland County Jail. After many objections, the city finally agreed to lend the jail's manpower. With the inmates' help, this elderly couple restored the ceilings and floors, replaced broken windows, replastered, and painted the three-story house. Many obstacles presented themselves, but after prayer and more light on the path, they always found a way. And God provided. Louise's husband, Claude, a noted artist, traded one of his paintings for appliances. Their daughter gave a new furnace. More funds were needed in order to open the shelter. For weeks, Louise went to churches of all faiths and returned with contributions of blankets, furniture, food, and money.

The night before Christmas Eve 1985, Friendship House opened its doors to serve the homeless with a graciousness and love their "guests" never dreamed of. We were there on a subsequent Christmas to help give a party for guests and serve dinner with our friend Louise. The Faith House for mothers and children eventually opened, and ever since then there has been a home for thousands of homeless people without charge—a place of healing, recovery, and hope that has endured past Louise's life on earth.

> If you can find a path with no obstacles, it probably doesn't lead anywhere.
>
> *Frank A. Clark*

Although your "steps" may be different from Louise's, the same principles apply—because God has a plan for you that he promises to reveal if you are looking, listening, and following his guidance: "I [the Lord] will instruct you and teach you the way you should go. I will counsel and guide you with My eye upon you," he says in Psalm 32:8 (AMP). God will provide the guidance and show you the steps to take, but he wants you to do your part to step out in faith.

Keep moving. Once your boat is in the water, don't get caught on the sandbar of discouragement. Keep moving forward. The old saying is true: You can't pilot a moored ship, especially one stuck in the dock. If God gives you an idea or a dream, get your sailboat in the water so the Holy Spirit can move your rudder and blow his wind on your sails. As one writer friend says, "I have yet to have an editor appear on my doorstep with a check and ask me for an article." We've got to plant seeds, move, prepare, work—doing our part and trusting God to do his. And one of the ways he does his part to direct us is by opening and closing doors.

Ask God to open and close doors, then be ready for both! That's how he moves your rudder—but when the closed doors or "NOs" come, keep going. Bounce back from discouragement—don't let it paralyze you. See rejection as redirection, not failure.

"I'm a door rattler," says my friend Norma Jean. She says, "If you want to close the door, Lord, that's fine. But I'm going to shake them all!" When she tries an idea that doesn't work, she doesn't stay flattened. "I've gotten knocked down a lot. Each time I get up a little quicker and run a little faster."

If you are looking for direction, read the Bible daily and let God speak to you through it. It's a major source of guidance. Read it to discover his will. The Bible is speaking today. And if you want to know God better, hear his direction, and learn his ways of living, open your Bible daily with great expectations. Before you read, ask: *What is this passage saying to me about God, about me? What do I hear God nudging me to do today?* The Bible "is more than a thing, it is a voice, a word, the very Word of the living God," says Tozer.[3]

Say yes in advance. This may sound strange, but it is an important key. If there is a decision to be made or a fork in the road and you are asking God to show you the way to go, sign on the dotted line of your contract with God in advance even before you know what he's going to have you do. Say, "Lord, I don't know what to do, but if you show me, I'll commit in advance to whatever you direct."

Does this sound scary or difficult? Are you afraid if you say yes that God will send you to some remote place you always dreaded or have you doing a job you hate? This may come from the notion that God is a mean killjoy just waiting to spoil our fun. Just the opposite is true of him!

> Things which eye has not seen and ear has not heard,
> And which have not entered the heart of man,
> All that God has prepared for those who love Him.
>
> 1 Corinthians 2:9 NASB

God's will is not a terrible or burdensome thing—it is the greatest thing to discover in all of life. It is the greatest adventure of a lifetime to walk with him and do what he has planned. And signing his contract in advance is a way of giving up any areas you are holding out on, areas like saying, "I'll go anywhere but not there." It is admitting that you are joyfully committing yourself to God and whatever he chooses for your life.

Even in uncertain situations, be encouraged that God is the best person to fill in the blank spaces because he is the only One who knows the future. We can't see around the corner like he can. He has the whole blueprint.

Sometimes I actually draw up a contract with God on a page in my journal. I draw lines and write out my commitment to follow God as he "fills in the blanks" to reveal his plan or the next step, and then I sign my name. He has never failed to direct me.

Let others join you on the journey. We're not on this trail alone, and God doesn't mean for us to be Lone Rangers. If we are open, he'll send people to encourage, speak truth, and be "Jesus with skin on." As part of the body of Christ, we need the other members and they need us. That's one of the reasons that we are all a combination of both strengths and weaknesses and why nobody is strong in every single area. God planned it this way so we need each other:

> Just as there are many parts to our bodies, so it is with Christ's body. We are all parts of it, and it takes every one of us to make it complete, for we each have different work to do. So we belong to each other, and each needs all the others. God has given each of us the ability to do certain things well.
>
> Romans 12:4–6 TLB

Prayer support and the counsel of trusted Christians on the adventure trail is crucial. We all go through times when we have been battered about in a storm, have lost someone or something dear to us, or feel alone. So we all need encouragement.

In addition, others who have gone before us in this adventure of faith can inspire us as we move along on the trail. Of course there are those in the Hall of Fame in Hebrews 11: Noah, who believed God and built the ark as commanded; Abraham, who left his home and went far away to the land God promised him; Jacob and Joseph, Moses and Joshua, and other people of great faith.

But also look at the lives of biblical women who could have been fearful but trusted God instead: Sarah, who because of her faith followed her husband and was able to become a mother in her old age; Esther, whom God brought into the palace of a king "for such a time as this" to save the nation of Israel. She responded with faith and dependence on God. Ruth, who though widowed at a young age, sought refuge under the wings of God. She left her own country and people to live with Naomi, her mother-in-law, in a foreign country. Deborah, Rahab, Mary, Elizabeth. They are all part of that great cloud of witnesses who are cheering us on in this adventure of Faith. Read their stories and remember you are not alone!

> In this life we need not carry our own burdens; the Lord is our burden-bearer, and on Him we can lay every care.
>
> *Hannah Whitall Smith*

Let God redeem your mistakes. It's inevitable that we are going to make mistakes on the adventure, even when we are purposing to follow God's will. But God turns ashes into beauty. He has a wonderful way of turning our mourning into joy and making bitter experiences sweet. He can redeem our mistakes and the mistakes of others to weave them into a pattern of good for our lives. Even what the enemy means for evil and destruction God uses for good—just look at the life of Joseph.

Maybe all you see is jagged lines across your life or a fragmented mess. Just as an artist can redeem a seemingly ruined painting with his brush strokes, how much more can God's love and power make beauty out of blunders, bring strength out of our weaknesses, change failures into successes.

We can move from "victim" or "failure" status when we give God our mistakes (confessing our own errors and asking for his help) and the mistakes of others who have hurt us.

We are hard-pressed on all sides, but we are never frustrated; we are puzzled, but never in despair. We are persecuted, but are never deserted: we may be knocked down but we are never knocked out! Every day we experience something of the death of Jesus, so that we may also show the power of the life of Jesus in these bodies of ours.

2 Corinthians 4:8–10 PHILLIPS

Don't let bitterness or envy, unforgiveness or self-pity eat away at your roots and weaken them. When my friend Flo Perkins went through a particularly difficult time, her daughter and two grandchildren were living with them. Her husband was deeply depressed and unable to work, and she was working long hours including weekends and holidays to support them all. Her strength was almost spent, and she wondered where God was.

Late one night a fierce winter rainstorm raged outside. As the wind howled and lightning flashed, Flo looked out in the dark to check on her young peach tree. She was troubled to see her little tree wrestling with the wind and rain. Back and forth, back and forth it went, bending nearly to the ground. The elements were wrestling with her peach tree as if for a prize, and it looked like the storm was winning the battle.

My little tree will surely be subdued and broken by morning, she thought, finally falling into a restless sleep. But the next morning, to her surprise, the storm had spent itself, but her peach tree stood tall and calm, basking in the morning sunlight. It seemed untroubled by the fierce battle it had experienced the night before. And somehow, seeing that the peach tree had survived the storm, Flo knew that whatever happened, God would be sufficient and provide the strength she needed to stand.

She was also reminded that trees are created to bend with the storm and bounce back unless they are diseased or improperly planted. Our roots, like those of a tree, must be deep in the soil if we are going to withstand the wind and storms, free from the disease of resentment or whatever would hinder us from following God and bending with the storms of life.

Hebrews 12:15 says, "See to it that no one comes short of the grace of God; that no root of bitterness springing up causes trouble, and by it many be defiled" (NASB). Keeping short accounts and forgiving quickly help keep our roots healthy and deeply rooted in God's love. And his grace will keep us just as he preserved the little peach tree and sustained Flo through this stormy, trying period of her life.

Look at problems as opportunities. Problems are inevitable. Just because you have them doesn't mean you've missed God's will. In the Chinese language, two characters make up the word *crisis*. One means "danger" and the other means "opportunity." Look at Daniel, Elijah, John the Baptist, and Paul and the problems they faced! Problems give us tremendous opportunities to grow, to stretch our faith, and to depend on God in a greater way. They cause our roots to go down deeper in Christ. Sometimes difficulties on the journey cause us to reevaluate, which can be useful. But hopefully they won't cause us to turn back or give up on the adventure of following God.

For almost every dream, idea, or goal God gives us, there is a *delay*, a time of *difficulty*, and even a *dead end* in which our situation deteriorates from difficult to impossible, and it looks hopeless for us to accomplish our goal. But these times are sent for a special purpose:[4] Paul says he and the brothers were crushed and overwhelmed in Asia, burdened beyond their strength. They even told themselves that it was the end. He goes on to say that they had this sense of impending disaster so that "we would not trust in ourselves, but in God who raises the dead; who delivered us from so great a peril of death, and will deliver us, He on whom we have set our hope" (2 Cor. 1:9–10 NASB).

Even in the midst of the problems, we can find peace on the adventure trail. It all depends on our perspective. Catherine Marshall told of a friend who had boarded a plane, waiting for takeoff. As she settled into her seat and buckled her seat belt, she noticed a strange thing. On one side of the airplane a sunset filled the entire sky with glorious color. But out of the window next to her seat, all she could see was a dark, threatening sky, with no sign of the beautiful sunset.

As the plane began to take off, a gentle voice spoke within her: "You have noticed the windows. Your life, too, will contain some happy, beautiful times but also some dark shadows. Here's a lesson I want to teach you to save you much heartache and allow you to abide in me with continual peace and joy.

"You see, it doesn't matter which window you look through; this plane is still going to Cleveland. So it is in your life. You have a choice. You can dwell on the gloomy picture. Or you can focus on the bright things and leave the dark, ominous situations to me. I alone can handle them anyway. And your final destination is not influenced by what you see or feel along the way."

If we learn this, we will be released and able to experience the peace that passes understanding on our adventure through life.[5]

Rejoice in today. If we are always thinking we'll be happy when we lose those ten pounds, or when our child gets potty trained, or gets through adolescence, or when we get the right job, or meet our goals, we may need to rethink our attitude— that day may never come. Don't miss out on the joy God has for you each day. Speak to your soul each morning and say, "This is the day the LORD has made. I will rejoice and be glad in it" (Ps. 118:24).

Then remind yourself throughout the day to celebrate. I have a card on my bathroom mirror that says, "Celebrate today! I have come that you might have life abundantly!" It reminds me on the darkest days to find something to celebrate: a gorgeous Oklahoma sunset, a scampering squirrel in the tree outside my window, a letter from a friend. Each day is a gift, and we can enjoy not only God and the marvelous love he has bestowed upon us but also his creation in all its changing seasons and beauty.

Peggy, a nurse and mother of three, has gone on three medical mission trips to Mexico and along the Amazon River. She teaches CPR classes for the American Red Cross and sets up first aid stations in the community. In her spare time she serves as an animal educator, taking zoo animals out to show to school-children, giving special tours at the zoos, and teaching classes about animals. For ten years she served each summer as a camp nurse for two hundred children in a camp. At forty-nine years old she tackled rock climbing, and she goes on mountain climbing and hiking adventures with the Sierra Club. What is her secret to living an adventurous life?

Every morning, Peggy looks at a poster on her closet door: "The size of your world is the size of your heart." She has found her heart is happiest learning, exploring, and being "out on the range." This former psychiatric nurse who once launched a clown ministry with her youth group says there are always more places to explore and more things she wants to do. Two other posters right by her breakfast table say, "Carpe Diem!" (Seize the Day) and "If life isn't an adventure, it's not living at all." These are visual reminders—like a breath of fresh air—to look for miracles, try something new, and grow!

Cast your cares every day. You can't soar like an eagle if you are carrying around a heavy backpack of cares and burdens. Because God cares for you (1 Peter 5:7), he invites you to turn those cares over to him. If you don't, you'll be too burdened down to continue on the adventure trail, or you'll get weary and drop out or burn out. God wants us to soar like the eagles, but we won't have the physical or spiritual energy to keep up with him unless we let him carry our cares, fears, and anxieties. We can choose by an act of the will yet depend on the Holy Spirit to help us cast each fear on the Lord. And we can trust his Spirit to enable us not to take it back.

> Life is a great adventure, or it is nothing. There is no such thing as security. Animals never experience it and children seldom do.
>
> *Helen Keller*

When you are doing your work and using your gifts for God's service, it is easy to think you have to carry the whole responsibility for the work yourself and need to worry about whether the results will please him. But that's when it is crucial to cast your cares! "But if the work is Christ's, the responsibility is His also, and we have no need to worry about results," says Hannah Whitall Smith. "The most effectual workers I know are those who do not feel the least anxiety about their work, but who commit it all to their Master. They ask Him to guide them moment by moment and trust Him implicitly for each moment's supply of wisdom and strength."[6]

Remember, God promises that no matter what happens on the adventure trail, nothing can separate us from his love:

For I am convinced that neither death, nor life, nor angels,
nor principalities, nor things present, nor things to come, nor
powers, nor height, nor depth, nor any other created thing,
will be able to separate us from the love of God, which is in
Christ Jesus our Lord.

Romans 8:38–39 NASB

No matter what difficulties arise on the journey, regardless of
whether you find success or failure (by the world's standards) in
your pursuit of your mission or in using your talents—God
couldn't love you any more than he does right now, and he'll never
quit loving you. He loved you so much he gave himself totally to
you and asks that you respond to his love. When you do commit
yourself to facing and overcoming your fears and living the adventure of following Christ, your life will be woven into God's plan
not only in this life but for all eternity.

Thank you, Father, that you
give us faith for our fears,
and your unfailing love for a lifetime;
you are rest for the weary
peace for the storm-tossed
strength for the powerless
and wisdom for all those who ask you.
You are exceedingly abundantly beyond
all we can ask or think—of blessing, help, and care!

The Lifeline of God's Word

Now the Lord is the Spirit, and where the Spirit of the Lord is,
there is liberty. But we all, with unveiled face, beholding as in
a mirror the glory of the Lord, are being transformed into the
same image from glory to glory, just as from the Lord, the Spirit.

2 Corinthians 3:17–19 NASB

*Lord, thank you that where you are, there is liberty! That you
desire to set me free me from every fear to worship you in Spirit and*

in truth and follow you as you lead me. Thank you that you are transforming me into your image from glory to glory!

> Have I not commanded you? Be strong and courageous! Do not tremble or be dismayed, for the LORD your God is with you wherever you go.

Joshua 1:9 NASB

Lord, help me be strong and courageous, not tremble or be dismayed, for you are with me wherever I go, and you will lead me with your light and truth.

For Discussion and Further Study

Fear is always better overcome with the support of a group instead of in isolation. That's why this Small Group Discussion Guide and Bible Study is provided. Fear and worry are particularly good topics to deal with in a group setting for several reasons. Often the fearful person feels she is the only one who struggles with these emotions. When she finds that others have similar fears, there's a great sense of relief. In addition, when the problems or burdens we are carrying alone are "divided" by having others discuss and pray with us about them, their sting is lessened and they are much less overwhelming. God didn't intend us to be isolated but to be part of a community of believers who love, support, and care for one another.

The questions are also ideal for individual reflection and journaling. They will help you take the material from the abstract to the concrete, help you apply the Scriptures and principles on overcoming fear to your own personal life, and move you from just thinking about fear or worry to taking action. Since the questions and exercises are optional and may be expanded upon as much as you'd like, there is not writing space for them in this study guide. So you will need a notebook or journal for recording the answers, discoveries, and insights God gives you.

How can you get the most out of this study? Consider taking one or more of the Scriptures and prayer promises in "Lifelines from God's Word" at the end of each chapter to memorize. When you memorize, meditate, and reflect on God's Word, it begins to renew your mind and transform your thinking and behavior (Rom. 12:2). You can also go deeper in God's Word by examining other Scriptures that are provided in this study.

What you need most as you start this study, besides your Bible, a notebook, and a pen, is a prayerful attitude and a heart open to the Holy Spirit and the healing and freedom he wants to bring into your life. Try reading a verse in different versions or paraphrases of the Bible. You may find commentaries, concordances, or other sources helpful guides if you desire a deeper understanding of Scripture. And most important, as you open your heart and life to the One who created you and loves you with an everlasting, unfailing love, ask him to guide you and give you a spirit of wisdom and revelation as you do this study. Bathe your study time in prayer, asking the Lord's Spirit to illuminate the Scripture and this book, to comfort your heart, and to transform your life.

Chapter 1: Facing Our Fear

1. What are some of your own personal telltale clues that you are afraid or anxious?

2. What do you do when you're in a state of anxiety or fear? Do you sleep too much or not enough? Become angry at the people around you? Get caught up in a frenzy of busyness? Try to control situations or others' behaviors?

3. What past or present experience keeps you from trusting God or tends to paralyze your faith?

4. What is an area of life in which you'd like to experience more peace and freedom and less anxiety?

5. What are some of the things that you fear the most? What fears have you overcome?

6. Read Psalm 55:22 and Hebrews 4:16. What burden do you need to give him today? Share with each other what your biggest burden is today and then together lift them up to God.

7. Read Hebrews 10:23–25 and talk about why we as believers need to gather together instead of being Lone Rangers in our spiritual journey. How can you minister to, support, and help one another?

Chapter 2: The High Cost of Fear

1. How could life be better if your fears are overcome?

2. What medical or physical problems have you observed in someone you know or in yourself that are the result of fear or worry? Read Proverbs 14:30 and discuss the by-product of a heart at peace.

3. What is the difference between healthy and unhealthy fears? What fears do you have that you would consider healthy? What fears do you have that you would consider destructive or that have had a negative effect on your life?

4. Review the list of devastating effects of fear listed in chapter 2 (on pages 20–22). List any of the negative effects of fear or positive effects of faith that you see at work in your life.

5. Share or write about a time fear caused you to say no to an opportunity or to harm or damage a relationship.

6. Read Isaiah 43:1–5.

a. What does the Lord tell us to do when we encounter trouble, difficulty, or oppression?

b. What does the Lord tell us about himself in these verses?

c. What do these verses tell us about how the Lord sees us (i.e., verse 1 says we are his creation and we belong to him)?

d. What promise is ours to claim in verse 5?

e. Take a few minutes to ask the Lord (or write a prayer in your journal) to help you place your trust in him, experience his tender love for you, and release your specific fears to him this day.

7. Read Isaiah 41:10–14 in two different Bible versions and discuss how this verse applies to any of the situations or fears you have mentioned in the questions above. In the midst of this fear-filled, anxiety-producing world, what is God saying to us in this verse? Why does he tell his people not to fear? What promise is contained in the passage?

Chapter 3: Centered on the Greatness of God

1. What circumstances in your life make it most difficult for you to focus on the Lord and praise him?

2. Read 1 Thessalonians 5:18.

a. What does the apostle Paul instruct us to do?

b. Share your experiences of giving thanks in difficulties.

c. Write a prayer of praise and thanksgiving to God, including how you see him working or moving in your present situation.

3. Read Romans 8:28.

a. What promise is ours to claim in this verse?

b. Who is able to claim this promise? Are you able to claim this promise?

4. Who in your life like Anne, the missionary from the China Inland Mission, has helped turn your focus from overwhelming problems to God or has encouraged you to praise God even when you didn't feel like it? If possible, ask this person how she kept her focus on the Lord while enduring difficult life circumstances and then share what you learned with the group.

5. What does Psalm 9:10 say about those who know God's name and nature? What is the promise in this verse for those who seek him?

6. Our fears decrease as we know God better, see him more clearly, and see our circumstances in the light of his Word and promises. Each of the many names of God in the Bible gives us a snapshot of another facet or character quality of God. In the ones that follow, write the name of God you discover in the verse. If you have experienced the facet of the Lord associated with one of the names, share the specific situation (i.e., I have experienced the Lord as my provider when . . .). If not, ask God to help you to experience him as your Creator, the God who is with you, your healer, or your provider.

> a. Exodus 15:26 (To dig a little deeper, read the whole chapter of Exodus 15 and list what you discover about God.)
>
> b. Genesis 22:1–8
>
> c. Judges 6:11–24 and John 16:33
>
> d. Genesis 28:3
>
> e. Genesis 21:33
>
> f. Matthew 1:22–23

7. Look up the following verses and identify the attribute of God you find there:

> a. Numbers 23:19
>
> b. Jeremiah 32:17, 27
>
> c. Psalm 139:7–12
>
> d. I Kings 8:27 and Isaiah 57:15

8. Write a prayer of praise and thanksgiving to God, including how you see him working in your present circumstances. If you are not aware of how he is at work, ask him to show you.

Chapter 4: Focusing on the Truth

1. a. Look up "truth" in a dictionary and write a brief definition.

   b. Read John 14:6. What does Jesus tell us about himself in this verse?

   c. Read 2 Timothy 3:16. What does this verse tell us about Scripture? What does "God-breathed" mean?

2. The Lord instructs us to "put on the belt of truth" as we meditate on God's Word and fill our minds with his truth (pages 39–40).

   a. In what ways have you "put on the belt of truth" this week? How have you been able to apply the Word to your life?

   b. Do you have any suggestions that may help others get started and/or continue spending time in the Word daily?

3. In his first televised address to the nation after the September 11 terrorist attacks, President Bush said, "Freedom and fear are at war." The same thing could be said about our lives spiritually.

   a. What area of your life is currently characterized by an overriding sense of freedom or fear?

   b. What steps might you take to release your fears and to rest more fully in the truth, in Jesus Christ?

4. Read Psalm 18:2.

   a. What does the Lord tell us about himself in this verse?

   b. What promise is ours to claim in this verse? What must we do in order to claim and experience the promise at work in our lives? This verse tells us the Lord is our protector in whom we can take refuge. Take a few minutes to ask God to help you take refuge in him this week.

5. All through the Bible, God says, "Fear not," so that we can believe and receive his promises in good times and difficult times. There's a promise and an instruction that follows every time God says, "Fear not." For example, in Joshua 8:1, the Lord said to Joshua, "Do not be afraid; do not be discouraged. Take the whole army with you, and go up and attack Ai." Just as God had commanded Joshua earlier to be strong, vigorous, and courageous, he promises his presence and empowering help: "Do not be terrified . . . for the Lord your God will be with you wherever you go" (Joshua 1:9 NIV). Look up other "fear nots" and notice what the Lord's command and promise are following the command:

a. 1 Chronicles 22:13

b. Luke 12:32

c. Deuteronomy 1:21

How can you apply the truth and encouragement in these verses to your situation?

6. What does Isaiah 26:3 say about the benefits of turning your thoughts to God and his Word? After making your own Peace Packet as described on pages 46–47 and using it each day, write down how it affects your life, thinking, and responses to situations. Then be ready to share the results with your group.

7. The Peace Packet and the verses and prayers at the close of each chapter give you an opportunity to pray God's Word. What have you experienced happening when you pray Scripture?

Chapter 5: From Panic to Peace

1. What pushes your panic button?

2. What is your "First Resource" when trouble comes? What do you do when panic strikes you? The next time you feel panicked, write down:

a. What you are thinking

b. What is happening to you at that time

    c. How you are responding to the situation

As you do this each time you become extremely anxious, you'll discover a "trigger" for your panic and a pattern for how you deal with it. Share what you've discovered with the group.

3. Write Philippians 4:6–9 in your own words. Verse 9 gives the fifth *P*—"Practice these things." Why is it important to keep giving God our fear or problem and to continue practicing the instruction of this passage in Philippians? Why can't we just hand it over once and be done with it?

4. Throughout the Gospels, we see that prayer was a priority for Jesus. Prayer was the avenue Jesus used to talk with and listen to his loving Father. In his moments of deep distress and anguish on the night of his betrayal, he turned once again to the Father in prayer. Read Matthew 26:36–45.

    a. Why did Jesus go to the Garden of Gethsemane on the Mount of Olives? What was his emotional and mental state at this time?

    b. Where do you go and what do you do when you're distressed?

    c. Who went with Jesus to Gethsemane, and what did he ask them to do for him? Did they do it? How did the Lord respond to their actions?

    d. When you're distressed and in need of prayer, do you invite others to support you by interceding on your behalf? If you've done so, how has this helped you? Or how could it have helped if you had asked for prayer support?

5. What steps will you take this week to let prayer become your first resource instead of your last resort?

6. Read Philippians 4:6–9 and John 14:27. After reviewing these verses, list what happens when we let go and make known to God our needs instead of fretting over them.

    a. For panic, he gives us _____

b. For worry, he gives us _____

7. Read Psalm 107:28–29. What do these verses say the Lord does when his people cry out in prayer to him in their trouble?

8. Reread 1 Peter 5:7, if possible in the Amplified Bible or another version. Imagine that Jesus comes to you and says, "Whatever concerns you or keeps you up late at night, I'll handle it. You can give it to me." What would you hand over? Write a prayer of thanksgiving for this wonderful invitation.

Chapter 6: Acceptance: The Door to Peace

1. Look up the word *acceptance* in the dictionary and write a definition in your own words. Then write three behaviors you learned from this chapter that do not characterize acceptance and three behaviors that do.

2. What are the things or people in your life that cause you the most frustration or that you have the most difficulty accepting? After listing these, find a verse from the Bible that addresses at least one of them.

3. When you experience a difficult time and can't control it, what are the barriers to your feeling peace and confidence in the midst of the situation?

4. The prophet Isaiah teaches us how we can know peace even in the midst of turmoil. Read Isaiah 26:3–4.

a. What kind of peace is promised to those whose minds are steadfast? Take a few minutes to reflect on your life and describe what it would be like to live in this kind of peace.

b. What does it mean to be steadfast?

c. What does it mean to trust? Who or what are you placing your trust in?

d. What allows those with steadfast minds to experience peace?

e. According to these verses, how long and for how much can we trust the Lord? Have you entrusted your cares to him?

5. Read Isaiah 30:15 and Psalm 94:19. What do these verses say about how we can find acceptance, have a quiet heart, and even experience hope and confidence in the midst of a trial that doesn't go away or change as we'd hoped?

6. Read Hebrews 13:5–6. In the Amplified Bible, the verse reads: "Be satisfied with your present circumstances and with what you have." What are three reasons you can find in these verses that explain why we can "be satisfied" or accept our situation?

7. If you have not placed your trust in the Lord as your Savior, provider, and source of peace, please do so by praying a simple prayer like, *Lord Jesus, I believe in you and I desire to place all my cares in your hands. I am a sinner and I ask you to forgive me. Thank you for this promise that as I trust in you and keep my mind steadfast on you, I will experience this perfect peace that only you can give! Help me to accept my circumstances and to fully trust you. Amen.*

Chapter 7: Overcoming Fears about Our Children

1. Psalm 127:3 says that children are a gift of the Lord. Write a prayer expressing to God why you are thankful for each of your kids. Include specific blessings you can give thanks for and things God has done in your children's and your family's life.

2. What in your children's lives do you feel is out of your control? How does this affect your ability to trust God with your kids?

3. Where are you in this process of coming to depend on God and his power to the point that you can stay in the turmoil yet be calm and unperplexed—related to whatever your kids are going through?

4. Share a time when you experienced fear or worry in regard to your child. How did you respond? What have you discovered in this chapter that you could apply when these kinds of things happen in the future?

5. If you are afraid to relinquish your child to God, what is holding you back? Pray that God's Spirit will reveal where this reluctance to trust comes from and ask him to give you the faith to trust him with your son or daughter.

6. Read Exodus 1:1–2:10.

a. What circumstances and threat caused Moses' mother to fear for him and his life? What was she able to do to help protect Moses when he was born? How did this reveal that she was a woman of courage?

b. What circumstances are causing you to fear for your child(ren) today? What threatens to bring harm to your kids today and in the future?

c. What can you do to protect them from these circumstances and threats? Are you doing these things? If not, would you pray and ask the Lord for wisdom to know what to do and the courage to step out in faith and do it?

d. When the time came that Moses' mother could no longer personally protect him, what did she do? How did this reveal that she was a woman of steadfast faith and courage?

e. What, if anything, is holding you back from being willing to place your little Moses in the Lord's protection, as Jochebed did with her son?

f. What blessings did Moses' mother experience as she carefully "let go" of Moses? What blessings might you miss if you choose to hold on rather than to let go and entrust your child(ren) to God?

7. Read Jeremiah 29:11 and spend a few minutes thanking the Lord for these promises. Pray these promises back to him for your children. For example:

Thank you, Lord, that you know all about the plans you have for _____. Thank you that it is your plan to prosper and not to harm _____. Lord, I thank you that your plans give _____ hope and a future.

Chapter 8: Overcoming Fears about Finances

1. If the financial "rug" has ever been pulled out from under you, share about how God provided and worked in this area of your life. What life lesson has he taught you in overcoming financial fears and problems? Who might he want you to share this with?

2. When fears or anxiety about finances plague you, what do you have a tendency to put off that causes your stress to increase?

3. Each of the following passages of Scripture gives instruction on handling our finances in both good and hard times. Look the verses up and write beside them what God is saying to you:

    a. Matthew 6:25–34

    b. Psalm 37:25

    c. Philippians 4:19

    d. James 1:17

4. Read Deuteronomy 29:5–6.

    a. How long did God lead the Israelites through the desert? What "financial desert" do you find yourself in at the moment? How long have you been there?

    b. How did God provide for his people's daily needs of clothing and nourishment? How long does it take for your shoes and clothes to wear out? Imagine what it would be like to have clothes and shoes that don't wear out for forty years!

c. What reason does God give for allowing the Israelites to wander in the desert for forty years while providing for them in unique ways?

d. If God can provide clothes and sandals that don't wear out after forty years of hard use, what might he do for you if you allow him to lead and provide for you, in his way and timing? Write down ways he has provided for you in the last week or month.

5. Giving back to God from our resources is a principle that runs throughout the Bible. What does each of these verses say about giving?

a. Malachi 3:10–12

b. Luke 6:38

c. 2 Corinthians 9:6–8

6. Making a Financial Peace Packet or adding verses that address money and God's provision to the packet you've already made can help you face challenging times (see chapter 4). Use verses from this chapter and the questions above, plus others you find in the Bible that apply to God's provision. There are hundreds throughout Scripture, so you have a lot to pick from! Share with your group how God's truth related to finances has changed your life.

7. If you are in a financial struggle, ask yourself, "What's the worst that could happen?" Then follow each scenario with the question, "Is God able?"

8. Write in your journal or notebook some of the ways God has blessed you in the past. Include little blessings (such as someone bought your lunch) and big blessings (such as an unexpected financial gift that met an important need). Pick one of these to share with your group. Write a prayer of thanksgiving to Jehovah-Jireh, the Lord your provider who is the giver of every good gift.

Chapter 9: Overcoming Fears That Harm Relationships

1. What relationship have you had the most difficulty trusting or fear has been a factor in? What coping strategies mentioned in this chapter have affected your relationships?

2. Read Ruth 1:1–22.

a. How long had Naomi lived in Moab when her sons died? Who grieved with her when her sons died?

b. As Naomi prepared to return to her homeland, who prepared to go with her?

c. Naomi was concerned that her daughters-in-law would remain unmarried if they went with her to Judah. How did Orpah and Ruth react to Naomi's concern? What did they decide to do?

d. What do you think Ruth saw in Naomi that caused her to be willing to put her fears aside and accompany her to a foreign land? While Orpah was going back to her gods, whose God was Ruth pursuing as she went to Bethlehem?

e. What do others see in you as they get to know you and spend time with you? Do you live your life in such a way that others see the Lord and desire to know him? Does your faith and love attract others to God?

3. What fears are harming relationships in your life now? In which one of these relationships do you need to leave your fears in the Lord's hands and take some steps toward reconciliation and restoration?

4. If Ruth had chosen to stay in familiar Moab, she would have missed a storehouse of blessings. Take a few minutes to ask the Lord to show you any actions you may need to take to ensure that you do not allow fear to cause you to miss out on the storehouse of blessings he has prepared for you. Write a

prayer asking God's empowering grace to fill each of your relationships.

5. First John 4:18 in the Message describes what happens when we are filled with God's love, a love that doesn't disappoint and is unconditional and everlasting: "There is no room in love for fear. Well-formed love banishes fear." How is God's love transforming your heart and relationships?

Chapter 10: Overcoming a Fear of Flying

1. What happens when people avoid doing the things that they fear instead of facing their fears by doing what makes them afraid? What has happened when you've confronted your fear head-on?

2. What have you avoided because you were scared? What fear keeps you from "flying" in life's great adventure?

3. Read Psalm 91 and memorize verses 1 and 2.

a. What must one do in order to experience peace and rest in the Lord? What is the promise of divine protection revealed in this psalm? In verses 14 and 15, what does God say he'll do when we call upon him in times of trouble?

b. What does it mean to "dwell in the shelter of the Most High"? Where do you "dwell" when you find yourself facing fear, particularly fear of flying?

c. If you have a fear of flying, what steps might you take to dwell in the shelter of the Most High as you prepare for your next flight?

4. Read Psalm 18:30. What does this verse say about where the strength will come from and who will provide your protection when God calls you to a "high place" where you once feared going? I encourage you to read *Hind's Feet on High Places*, Hannah Hurnard's classic book that has tremendous

wisdom and truth about facing and overcoming life's challenges, especially fear, to follow where God leads us.

5. Where or in what is your true security, whether you're in an airplane, train, car, or on foot? See Proverbs 21:31 and Habakkuk 3:19.

6. When you face a fear with God, certain positive things happen in your relationship with him. You may feel closer to the Lord; your trust level may jump a few notches. What have you experienced when the Lord has led you through a scary or dangerous situation? How did it affect your relationship with him?

7. Read Psalm 139 and make a list of reasons why you should give over control of your life, travel, and future to God. What two things does this psalm say God does for us with his hand? How does it make you feel to know that the God of all creation does this for you?

Chapter 11: Overcoming Childhood Fears

1. What were some of your childhood fears that may have been dragged into adulthood? Is there a childish pattern that has remained?

2. How did you react when you were young and afraid of something?

3. What fear, if any, do you think has been passed on to you from a parent or family member?

4. Overcoming childhood fears is a two-sided equation. The Bible helps us to understand our part of that equation, as well as God's part.

God's Part

Read Luke 1:37. What does this verse tell us about God? What does this verse tell us about our childhood fears in light of this great truth about God?

Our Part

Read John 5:24; 6:47. What must we do to gain access to all that the Lord has planned for our lives? What do we receive when we believe in Jesus? When does eternal life begin? How does this impact your life now?

5. Read Mark 9:13–42, paying close attention to verses 21–24.

a. Did the father initially believe in Jesus and in his healing power? What did it take for the father to believe? What were Jesus' words? How did the father respond?

b. Do you believe that Jesus is able to give you victory over childhood fears? If so, praise and thank the Lord for his power and love. If you are not sure, perhaps you, like the father, need to ask Jesus to help you overcome your unbelief. If you do, he will be faithful to reveal himself to you and to answer your prayer.

6. Read Matthew 7:7–8.

a. What does Jesus command us to do? What is the result of doing these things by faith in Christ?

b. What do you think would happen if you were to ask the Lord to help you overcome your childhood fears by seeking his will and way with perseverance?

c. What step of faith will you take this week to believe, ask, seek, and knock?

Chapter 12: Overcoming a Fear of Failure

1. Read Exodus 4:10–17.

a. How did Moses describe his speaking skills? Was he comfortable with what the Lord was asking him to do? How did he respond to the Lord's request that he speak on the Lord's behalf?

b. How do you respond when the Lord provides opportunities and "calls" you to serve him in an area that you are not comfortable with? How has fear derailed you from responding to God's opportunities or moving forward with his plan for your life?

2. According to these verses, where do our gifts and talents come from? How were you creatively and uniquely designed by God to bless others? (Skim the passages where spiritual gifts are described and add these to your "natural" skills: 1 Corinthians 12:7–11; Ephesians 4:11–13; 1 Peter 4:10–11; Romans 12:6–8.) Which gifts have you been hiding under a bushel due to fear of failure instead of developing and using?

3. What things have caused you to fear failure or hold back on pursuing your dream?

4. How do you think the Lord wants to use your gifts and talents? Are you willing to serve him, or are you hoping (like Moses) that God will ask someone else to do it?

5. When we respond in obedience to what the Lord asks us to do, he promises to help us and teach us. Note the evidences of God's help in verses 14–17. Can you share about a time when the Lord did this for you? If you are struggling with fear about something you believe the Lord wants you to do, take a few minutes right now to pray (individually, by writing a prayer, or with your group) and ask the Lord to help you and to teach you as you step out in faith and obedience.

6. Fill in the blank: *When I* _____, *I am filled with joy or sense God's pleasure.* This can be a strong clue that you're to use this for God's purpose. What passion has God put into your heart to pursue at this season of life?

7. Jeremiah 29:11 is a helpful, uplifting verse to memorize and believe for your own life. What does this verse tell us about the conditions for living a life with a bright future and hope?

Chapter 13: Overcoming Fears Concerning Health

1. Read Psalm 20:7. What do those who do not trust in the Lord place their trust in? What are some of the "chariots" and "horses" people put their trust in today? What medical "chariots" and "horses" are you tempted to place your trust in?

2. Read Psalm 56:3–4.

   a. What two things does David do when he is afraid?

   b. What does he experience as a result of doing these things?

3. Read Psalm 122:7. Can you share about a time when you were afraid of receiving some bad news from a doctor? How did you deal with that fear? How can we apply the wisdom from this verse to responding to a negative diagnosis or bad medical news?

4. Read Psalm 10:17; 55:22. What are we to do with our cares and concerns about any area of life, including health issues? What does God do when he hears the desires of the afflicted?

5. Proverbs 17:22 says a merry heart is good medicine. How does humor help overcome fear or anxiety about health problems? How could you incorporate humor into your life? Brainstorm as a group and try one of the strategies this week. Pray for a restored sense of humor and a merry heart if yours has disappeared.

6. Read 2 Corinthians 12:9; Ezekiel 37:23; Romans 8:1–4. What a wonderful thing that God's grace allows us to be transparent about our weakness and open to receiving his strength. For what weakness do you need God's strength in this season?

7. Who would be your prayer team if you became physically ill? What suffering person could you be praying for? See James 5:13–18. What does this tell us about praying for the sick?

8. Second Corinthians 1:3–4 gives us instructions on what to do with the comfort we've been given in our time of need. How have you been helped or comforted by someone when

you were suffering? What is something you have learned that you could use to encourage or aid another person?

9. Spiritual growth in a time of physical illness can be accelerated. It can be a wake-up call or a doorway to experience God in deeper intimacy. How have you experienced this in your own life or observed it in someone you know?

Chapter 14: Overcoming Fears in the Midst of Disaster

1. Are you living (or have you lived) through a traumatic experience, an uncontrollable situation, or a "storm"? Write down what it is and how you have responded to it.

2. Sometimes our fears about what might happen are worse than the reality. Just as Cyndi experienced, sometimes 98 percent of what we worry about comes true; the other 2 percent happens, and we can't control it anyway. What are some things that you've worried about that have never happened?

3. What does it mean to "look from the top" as Song of Solomon 4:8 says? How can you apply this to your situation or to a future calamity?

4. To whom does Psalm 46 say we are to turn when everything is shaken and all our sources of security, humanly speaking, fail us? Why is this a sure refuge in an insecure world? Memorize verse 10 of Psalm 46. How can you put this into practice this week?

5. Look up one of the following Scriptures and share with your group what we can learn about God's intervention, God's power being displayed, or God's purpose being accomplished.

Joseph—Genesis 39–47

Jehoshaphat—2 Chronicles 20

David—2 Chronicles 18–22

Hezekiah—2 Kings 18–19

Ruth—Ruth 1–4

Hannah—1 Samuel 1–3

Esther—Esther 1–10

Paul—Acts 16–19

6. One of the best cures for fear is to help others in need. To whom could you reach out, assist, or comfort in this season of life?

7. What steps will you take this week to put your faith, trust, and hope in the Lord alone for what you are presently facing or what may be ahead?

Epilogue: Living the Adventure

1. Read Philippians 3:10–14.

   a. According to Paul, what is the secret to living a victorious life?

   b. What does it mean to experience the "power of Christ's resurrection"?

   c. What is that high calling he may be wanting you to pursue or persevere in?

2. Read 2 Corinthians 2:14.

   a. What does this verse tell us about how God leads us as we "live the adventure"? How often does he lead us in this way? In whom does he lead us in "triumphal procession"?

   b. What does it mean to be led in triumphal procession in Christ? In what ways have you experienced this triumphal procession? If you are not experiencing it, will you put your trust in Christ and ask him to lead you triumphantly?

   c. How does the Lord use us when we are following him? What does it mean to "spread everywhere the fragrance of the knowledge of him"? What fragrance are you spreading everywhere as you live the adventure? Write a prayer telling him you are willing to follow where he leads and ask for the courage to do so.

3. When have you followed God's light on your path? When you took a step of faith, what was the result? How did he meet you?

4. When has your adventure been bogged down by fear or worry? What principles did you discover in this chapter or in previous chapters that can help you pursue your own adventure with God, moving out of your comfort zone to follow his leading?

5. Memorize Romans 8:36–39. How could you apply the truth of this passage to your life?

6. Share about a time when a problem became an opportunity, when God redeemed a mistake you made, or when what looked like a failure turned into something beautiful that God used in the tapestry of your life.

7. What are some of the simple, everyday things you could celebrate and enjoy today regardless of the stresses or difficulties you are experiencing? Write these in your journal and share with the group.

"May the God of hope fill you with all joy and peace as you trust in him, so that you may overflow with hope by the power of the Holy Spirit."

Romans 15:13

Notes

Chapter 2: The High Cost of Fear

1. Paul Tournier, quoted in Keith Miller and Bruce Larson, *The Edge of Adventure* (Waco: Word, 1976), 180.

Chapter 3: Centered on the Greatness of God

1. Corrie ten Boom, *Reflections of God's Glory* (Grand Rapids: Zondervan, 1999), 91–92.
2. Ruth Myers, *31 Days of Praise* (Singapore: The Navigators, 1992), 19.
3. Ibid.
4. Fern Nichols, "Heart to Heart," volume 7 (1995), 1.
5. Dave Shive, "You've Got to Fear Somebody," *Discipleship Journal* 130 (July/August 2002): 44.

Chapter 4: Focusing on the Truth

1. Edith Schaeffer, "God's Definition of Faith," in *One Holy Passion*, ed. Judith Couchman (Colorado Springs: Waterbrook Press, 1998), 153–54.
2. Rick Joyner, "Fighting the Good Fight," www.morningstarministries .org (10 October 2001), 1.
3. This story is adapted from "Bravehearts: My Journey through Fear" by Grace Saen in *Discipleship Journal*, issue 130, 2002, page 37. Used by permission.
4. Judson Cornwall, *Praying the Scriptures* (Lake Mary, Fla.: Creation House, 1988), 10–11.

Chapter 5: From Panic to Peace

1. Robert Jamieson, quoted in Cynthia Heald's *Abiding in Christ* (Colorado Springs: NavPress, 1995), 44.

Chapter 6: Acceptance: The Door to Peace

1. Hannah Hurnard, *Hind's Feet on High Places* (Wheaton: Tyndale House, 1975), 11–12.
2. Francois Fénelon, *Let Go* (Springdale, Pa.: Whitaker House, 1973), 3.
3. David Wilkerson, "Bringing Christ into Your Crisis," Times Square Church Pulpit Series (1 January 1996), 4.
4. Catherine Marshall, *Adventures in Prayer* (New York: Ballantine, 1975), 63.
5. Andrew Murray, quoted in *The New Encyclopedia of Christian Quotations* (Grand Rapids: Baker, 2000), 224.

Chapter 7: Overcoming Fears about Our Children

1. Karen Burton Mains, "Sacrificing Our Isaacs," in *One Holy Passion,* 138.

Chapter 9: Overcoming Fears That Harm Relationships

1. Barbara Sullivan, *The Control Trap* (Minneapolis: Bethany, 1991), 79, 81.
2. Stephen Arterburn, Dr. Paul Meier, and Dr. Robert Wise, *Fear Less for Life* (Nashville: Thomas Nelson, 2002), 57.
3. Ibid., 58.
4. Bruce Larson, *Living beyond Our Fears: Discovering Life When You're Scared to Death* (New York: HarperSanFransisco, 1990), 128.
5. Ibid., 150.
6. "In Your Arms of Love," Mercy Publishing, 1991.
7. A. W. Tozer, *Whatever Happened to Worship?* (Camp Hill, Pa.: Christian Publications, Inc., 1982), 91.
8. The term "Christ-conscious" is adapted from Larson, *Living beyond Our Fears,* 131.

Chapter 10: Overcoming a Fear of Flying

1. Hurnard, *Hind's Feet on High Places,* 11–12.
2. Ibid., 127.
3. Elisabeth Elliot, *Keep a Quiet Heart* (Ann Arbor, Mich.: Servant Publications, 1995), 53.
4. Arterburn, Meier, and Wise, *Fear Less for Life,* 158–59.

5. Cynthia Heald, "Mirrors," also quoted in Cynthia Heald, *Abiding in Christ*, 83.

6. Don Gossett, *How to Conquer Fear* (Springdale, Pa.: Whitaker House, 1981), 132.

Chapter 11: Overcoming Childhood Fears

1. Robert McGee, *The Search for Freedom* (Ann Arbor, Mich.: Servant Publications, 1995), 65.

2. Sullivan, *The Control Trap*, 75.

3. Carol Kent, *Tame Your Fears* (Colorado Springs: NavPress, 1993), 196.

4. McGee, *Search for Freedom*, 65.

5. Arterburn, Meier, and Wise, *Fear Less for Life*, 132–33.

Chapter 12: Overcoming a Fear of Failure

1. Reported by Robert L. Crandall, "Vantage Point," *American Way*, 1 May 1994, 8.

2. Dale Carnegie, *The Quick and Easy Way to Effective Speaking* (Garden City, N.Y.: Dale Carnegie & Associates, Inc., 1962), 26.

3. This story is adapted from *God Just Showed Up* by Linda Watkins, Moody Press, copyright 2001, pages 197–206. Used with permission.

4. Greg Alberico, "The Fear of Failure," *Living with Teenagers*, September 2002, 28–30.

5. Carnegie, *Quick and Easy Way*, 26.

Chapter 13: Overcoming Fears Concerning Health

1. Larson, *Living beyond Our Fears*, 99.

Chapter 14: Overcoming Fears in the Midst of Disaster

1. Larry Jones, "Controlling the Uncontrollable," Oklahoma City: Feed the Children, 1995, 2.

2. Amy Carmichael, *Edges of His Ways* (Fort Washington, Pa: Christian Literature Crusade, 1988), 175.

3. Lisa Beamer, *Let's Roll* (Wheaton: Tyndale House, 2002), 300–301.

4. Ibid.

5. From Cathy Herndon's "Peace Packet" (Oklahoma City, 1995), 12.

6. Cyndi Curry, "Lord, I Don't Want to Be Here," *Brio & Beyond Magazine*, October 2002, 29.

7. Pam Vredevelt, *Letting Go of Worry and Anxiety* (Sisters, Ore.: Multnomah, 2001), 86–87, 89.

8. Gossett, *How to Conquer Fear*, 86–87.

Epilogue: Living the Adventure

1. Terry Crist, "Don't Fear Transition," *SpiritLed Woman*, June/July 2001, 16.

2. Oswald Chambers, *My Utmost for His Highest*, rev. ed., ed. James Reimann (Nashville: Thomas Nelson, 1995), January 31.

3. A. W. Tozer, *Pursuit of God* (Camp Hill, Pa.: Christian Publications, Inc., 1982), 82.

4. Rick Warren, *Fax of Life* (Mission Viejo, Calif.: self-published, 6 January 1996).

5. Catherine Marshall in *Touching the Heart of God*, quoted in *Christianity Today*, 15 May 1995, 36.

6. Hannah Whitall Smith, *God Is Enough* (New York: Ballantine, 1986), 103.

Cheri Fuller is an inspirational speaker and the author of thirty books, including the best-selling *When Mothers Pray*. Winner of the Gold Medallion award for *Extraordinary Kids* (coauthored with Louise Tucker Jones) and the finalist for *When Families Pray*, Fuller is a prolific author who has written hundreds of articles for *Focus on the Family, Moody, CHILD, Family Circle, Pray!* magazine, and many others. She is a contributing editor for *Today's Christian Woman*, and her web site, www.CheriFuller .com, features her column, "Mothering by Heart," and information on her speaking and resources. She and her husband live in Oklahoma.